The Relationship

Of

THE HOLY SPIRIT

And

THE CHRISTIAN

OTHER BOOKS BY EDMUND R. McDAVID III

Let God Speak: And Let Us Listen
ISBN 0-9630447-1-0

God's Guarantee: Are You Covered By It?
ISBN 0-9630447-3-7

Infant Salvation And The Age Of Accountability
What Does The Bible Teach?
ISBN 0-9630447-4-5

Hope Publishing Company
P. O. Box 131447
Birmingham, Alabama 35213
(205) 871-1426

The Relationship

Of

THE HOLY SPIRIT

And

THE CHRISTIAN

The Spirit's work in the Christian
and through the Christian.

Edmund R. McDavid III

Hope Publishing Company
P. O Box 131447
Birmingham, Alabama 35213
(205) 871-1426

The Relationship
Of
The Holy Spirit
And
The Christian

Scripture taken from the Holy Bible: New International
Version. Copyright @1973, 1978, 1984 by the International
Bible Society.

First printing 2006

ISBN 0-9630447-5-3

Published by: Hope Publishing Company
            P. O. Box 131447
            Birmingham, AL 35213
            (205) 871-1426

Printed in the United States of America

Cover Design by Jennifer Bromberg Joseph

DEDICATION

To my grandchildren: Taylor Joseph and his wife Jennifer, Edmund Joseph, Lyndsay Rutherford and her husband Jeff, and Michael McDavid. All of you professed to repent and trust Christ at an early age. It is my prayer that your walk with the Lord through the years will prove your profession to be genuine. I am convinced it will. I love you all.

And to my great-granddaughter Maggie Joseph, daughter of Taylor and Jenn. You are such a wonderful little bundle of joy. It is my prayer that by the time you are able to read this you will have realized that you need a savior and will have repented and trusted Christ to save you. I love you.

ACKNOWLEDGMENTS

A special thanks to Peg, my sweet wife of 55 years. She did again what she did before with my first three books: she put it on the computer, made the numerous changes, additions, and deletions, and printed a "camera ready" product.

I appreciate very much the work of what we jokingly call my "Editorial Board." The board is comprised of my wife Peg, my son Mike McDavid and his wife Mikelyn, my daughter Peggy Joseph and her husband Thomas, and my grandchildren: Taylor Joseph and his wife Jennifer, Edmund Joseph, Lyndsay Rutherford and her husband Jeff, and Michael McDavid. They read the "rough manuscript" and gave me their thoughts and recommended changes. My cousin Jack McDavid also read the manuscript and gave me his thoughts and ideas. By God's grace their work and their prayers contributed greatly to the finished book.

CONTENTS

Preface

10 **Teach me to do your will, for you are my God; may your good Spirit lead me on level ground.** (Psalm 143:10).

PREFACE

I can remember my younger sister Mitzi, who some years ago was called home to be with the Lord, telling me and my wife, Peg, that we needed to have a personal relationship with Jesus Christ. However, Peg and I were content with our understanding of who Jesus was and saw no need to be concerned. But, Mitzi continued from time to time to bring up the idea of a personal relationship with Christ. We did not understand what she meant, but we finally decided to find out. And find out we did. We learned that to go to heaven when we died we needed to do much more than give intellectual accent to the fact that Jesus is Savior and Lord. My testimony is in the back of this book; however, I mention the above to illustrate how easy it is as a non-Christian to let knowing <u>about</u> Christ cause you to neglect seeking a personal relationship with Him.

In the same manner many Christians let knowing <u>about</u> the Holy Spirit cause them to neglect seeking a more meaningful relationship with Him.

When I first became a Christian, I did not know anything about the Holy Spirit. I had heard the name but that was it. I did not know that I was indwelt by the Holy Spirit; nor did I know that it was only through my relationship with the Holy Spirit that I could live the Christian life. I have now learned that as I had to repent and trust Christ to become a Christian, I now have to submit to and trust the Holy Spirit to enable and empower me to live the Christian life. This personal relationship between the Holy Spirit and the Christian is vital in every way. The work of the Holy Spirit in and through the Christian is not taught nearly as much as it should be in the church today. It is my hope that God will use this book to help many Christians begin to live victorious, Spirit-controlled lives.

Ed McDavid III
January 2006

EXAMINE YOURSELF,
ARE YOU A CHRISTIAN?

As I begin to write about the relationship of the Holy Spirit and the Christian, I realize there are a number of people who think they are Christians but they really are not. This leads to a false sense of security concerning salvation. Many people who claim to be Christians — whether they are Catholic or Protestant, go to church or not — would be in the same boat I was in at one time. They see themselves as earning the right to go to heaven when they die. They are aware that they are not perfect and that many people do better than they do; yet they feel their good outweighs their bad and that God will accept them as worthy of heaven. I thought this way until I was forty-one years of age. If I had died before I learned the truth, I would have gone straight to hell. You can imagine how grateful I am to God that I learned the truth before it was too late.

The Bible makes it clear that everyone who claims to be a Christian should examine themselves to be sure that they really are a Christian — that their salvation is real.

5 Examine yourselves to see whether you are in the faith; test yourselves. Do you not realize that Christ Jesus is in you—unless, of course, you fail the test?
(2 Corinthians 13:5).

There are three reasons in particular why we should examine ourselves:

1. We are told to do this in Scripture.

2. The assurance of our salvation is strengthened if we find that our walk lines up with our talk. Of course, none of us are perfect and we will find areas where we need to improve.
3. If we find we are not Christians then we have the opportunity to correct the situation before it's too late. If we believe we are Christians, but never examine ourselves, we could lead a self-deceived life and find ourselves in hell for eternity.

Checking ourselves to be sure that we are truly Christians is not something to take lightly or do in a hurry. We must be serious about it and be honest with ourselves. We must look at more than what we say. We need to look at what we think and what we do. We do not want to deceive ourselves by professing Christ as Savior and Lord, going to church on Sunday, and thinking that is all there is to being a Christian. If we are truly Christians we will do more than hear what the Bible says – we will try to do what the Bible says.

> **22 Do not merely listen to the word, and so deceive yourselves. Do what it says.** (James 1:22).

> **24 "Therefore everyone who hears these words of mine and puts them into practice is like a wise man who built his house on the rock. 25 The rain came down, the streams rose, and the winds blew and beat against that house; yet it did not fall, because it had its foundation on the rock. 26 But everyone who hears these words of mine and does not put them into practice is like a foolish man who built his house on sand. 27 The rain came down, the streams rose, and the winds blew and beat against that house, and it fell with a great crash."**
> (Matthew 7:24-27).

The Bible has a number of examples of people who appear to be Christians but later we find they are not. One example is the Parable of the Sower:

1 That same day Jesus went out of the house and sat by the lake. 2 Such large crowds gathered around him that he got into a boat and sat in it, while all the people stood on the shore. 3 Then he told them many things in parables, saying: "A farmer went out to sow his seed. 4 As he was scattering the seed, some fell along the path, and the birds came and ate it up. 5 Some fell on rocky places, where it did not have much soil. It sprang up quickly, because the soil was shallow. 6 But when the sun came up, the plants were scorched, and they withered because they had no root. 7 Other seed fell among thorns, which grew up and choked the plants. 8 Still other seed fell on good soil, where it produced a crop—a hundred, sixty or thirty times what was sown. 9 He who has ears let him hear." (Matthew 13:1-9).

We see that the sower is scattering the Word of God on the path, on rocky places, among thorns, and on good soil. Notice that of the four types of people receiving the Word, two of them appear to be Christians for a time, but later it is shown by their lives that they are not. Only the fourth example is the true Christian, and we know him from the fruit he produces.

18 "Listen then to what the parable of the sower means: 19 When anyone hears the message about the kingdom and does not understand it, the evil one comes and snatches away what was sown in his heart. This is the seed sown along the path. 20 The one who received the seed that fell on rocky places is the man who hears the word and at once receives it with joy. 21 But since he has no root, he lasts only a short time. When trouble or persecution comes because of the word, he quickly falls away. 22 The one who received the seed that fell among the thorns is the man who hears the word, but the worries of this life and the deceitfulness of wealth choke it, making it unfruitful. 23 But the one who received the seed that fell on good soil is the man who hears the word and understands it. He produces a crop, yielding a hundred, sixty or thirty times what was sown." (Matthew 13:18-23).

The Bible is very clear — fruit is an all-important validation that one is a Christian. Some Christians produce more fruit than others, but all who are truly Christians will produce fruit.

> 1 "I am the true vine, and my Father is the gardener. 2 He cuts off every branch in me that bears no fruit, while every branch that does bear fruit he prunes so that it will be even more fruitful. 3 You are already clean because of the word I have spoken to you. 4 Remain in me, and I will remain in you. No branch can bear fruit by itself; it must remain in the vine. Neither can you bear fruit unless you remain in me. 5 "I am the vine; you are the branches. If a man remains in me and I in him, he will bear much fruit; apart from me you can do nothing. 6 If anyone does not remain in me, he is like a branch that is thrown away and withers; such branches are picked up, thrown into the fire and burned. 7 If you remain in me and my words remain in you, ask whatever you wish, and it will be given you. 8 This is to my Father's glory, that you bear much fruit, showing yourselves to be my disciples. (John 15:1-8).

> 10 And we pray this in order that you may live a life worthy of the Lord and may please him in every way: bearing fruit in every good work, growing in the knowledge of God... (Colossians 1:10).

As you examine yourself, ask the question: Am I producing fruit that brings God glory? If I am not, then why am I not? Remember, it is not a matter of producing fruit to get saved, and it is not a matter of producing fruit to stay saved. It is a matter of producing fruit because you are saved. This is how Christians glorify God.

> 8 This is to my Father's glory, that you bear much fruit, showing yourselves to be my disciples. (John 15:8).

As we examine ourselves, the following are important questions to ask:

1. Do I have a personal relationship with Christ?
2. Can I give a Christian testimony as to how I was saved?
3. Do I believe the Bible?
4. Do I love Jesus Christ?
5. Have I "counted the cost" of being a Christian?
6. Do I exhibit the fruit of the Spirit?
7. Does God's Spirit testify to me that I am a Christian?
8. Is the purpose of my life to glorify God?
9. Am I doing the work God called me to do?
10. Do I love fellow Christians?

Let us look at each of these questions to see what light they may shed on whether or not we are Christians.

1. Do I have a personal relationship with Christ? If you have a personal relationship with Christ, this question will make sense to you. If you don't have a personal relationship with Christ, this question will raise another question: What do you mean by "personal relationship?" It means exactly "what it says", it is a personal relationship between you and Christ. You don't just know about Christ — you actually know Christ. You speak to Him through thoughts and prayers and He speaks to you through the Bible and the promptings of the Holy Spirit. The Bible teaches that the Christian is in Christ and Christ is in the Christian. Is that the case with you?

2. Can I give a Christian testimony? Can I tell someone how I was saved? This is not your idea of how to be saved but God's plan of salvation found in the Bible. If you can't show someone from the Bible how to be saved, what makes you think that you are saved?

3. Do I believe the Bible? I don't mean the quick "yes" that so many people give when asked that question. I mean a thought through "yes" or "no". We are not talking about just the plan of salvation — we are talking about the entire Bible. Do you believe the miracles, the prophecies, and what the Bible says about Adam and Eve and creation? Do you believe what the Bible says about Samson?

> [3] Samson said to them, "This time I have a right to get even with the Philistines; I will really harm them." [4] So he went out and caught three hundred foxes and tied them tail to tail in pairs. He then fastened a torch to every pair of tails, [5] lit the torches and let the foxes loose in the standing grain of the Philistines. He burned up the shocks and standing grain, together with the vineyards and olive groves.
> (Judges 15:3-5).

> [14] As he approached Lehi, the Philistines came toward him shouting. The Spirit of the LORD came upon him in power. The ropes on his arms became like charred flax, and the bindings dropped from his hands. [15] Finding a fresh jawbone of a donkey, he grabbed it and struck down a thousand men.
> (Judges 15:14-15).

What about the prophet Elisha?

> [23] From there Elisha went up to Bethel. As he was walking along the road, some youths came out of the town and jeered at him. "Go on up, you baldhead!" they said. "Go on up, you baldhead!" [24] He turned around, looked at them and called down a curse on them in the name of the LORD. Then two bears came out of the woods and mauled forty-two of the youths. [25] And he went on to Mount Carmel and from there returned to Samaria.
> (2 Kings 2:23-25)

You say you believe the Bible — do you believe what the above verses say? All three passages sound preposterous to us today. But this is today and that was then.

God did many things in the earlier years of His creation that we either have to disbelieve or believe and marvel at. Could the God who created everything out of nothing by just speaking it into existence cause the three hundred foxes to be caught by Samson, or cause two bears to come out of the woods and maul forty-two youths? Certainly He could. Did He not cause all the animals on Noah's ark to come and enter the ark? Yes, He did.

> [15] Pairs of all creatures that have the breath of life in them came to Noah and entered the ark.
> (Genesis 7:15).

Giving Samson the strength and ability to kill a thousand men was easy for God. God is all-powerful — with Him nothing is impossible.

> [37] For nothing is impossible with God." (Luke 1:37).

4. Do I love Jesus Christ? Love for Christ is the inseparable companion of faith. There is no one in heaven that does not love Christ, and no one will get to heaven that does not love Him.

> [28] And we know that in all things God works for the good of those who love him, who have been called according to his purpose. (Romans 8:28).

> [24] Grace to all who love our Lord Jesus Christ with an undying love. (Ephesians 6:24).

Christ asked Peter "Do you love me?" We must ask ourselves "Do I truly love Christ?" The non-Christian does not love Christ, and if he says he does he is deceiving himself. The unsaved man, whether he is Jew or Gentile, is an enemy of God. All Christians were enemies of God before they were saved — before they were reconciled to God. Paul makes that clear in his letter to the church at Rome.

> [10] For if, when we were God's enemies, we were reconciled to him through the death of his Son, how much more, having been reconciled, shall we be saved through his life! (Romans 5:10)

Some Pharisees claimed God as their father, but Christ told them their father was the devil. Satan is the father of all who don't belong to Christ, Jew or Gentile — all the unsaved.

> [42] Jesus said to them, "If God were your Father, you would love me, for I came from God and now am here. I have not come on my own; but he sent me. [43] Why is my language not clear to you? Because you are unable to hear what I say. [44] You belong to your father, the devil, and you want to carry out your father's desire. (John 8:42-44a)

I believe it is easier to measure our love for Christ than it is to measure our faith in Christ. You might say that our love for Christ is an indicator of whether or not we are truly trusting Christ to save us. How do we measure our love? Words themselves are not sufficient.

> [18] Dear children, let us not love with words or tongue but with actions and in truth. (1 John 3:18)

Many men talk a good game, but as the old saying goes "talk is cheap." God who knows everything knows our hearts.

> [13] The Lord says: "These people come near to me with their mouth and honor me with their lips, but their hearts are far from me. Their worship of me is made up only of rules taught by men. (Isaiah 29:13).

> [31] My people come to you, as they usually do, and sit before you to listen to your words, but they do not put them into practice. With their mouths they express devotion, but their hearts are greedy for unjust gain. (Ezekiel 33:31).

True love for Christ is found in one who is obedient to Christ.

> [3] This is love for God: to obey his commands. And his commands are not burdensome... (1 John 5:3).

> [23] Jesus replied, "If anyone loves me, he will obey my teaching. My Father will love him, and we will come to him and make our home with him. [24] He who does not love me will not obey my teaching. These words you hear are not my own; they belong to the Father who sent me. (John 14:23-24).

> [21] Dear friends, if our hearts do not condemn us, we have confidence before God [22] and receive from him anything we ask, because we obey his commands and do what pleases him. (1 John 3:21-22).

We should feel our love for Christ in our hearts. Think of the way we feel our love for a child, a parent, a brother or sister, a wife or husband. We should feel much more love for Christ than we do for any of these. The question is, do we? Do we really love Him much more than anyone or anything? Are we willing to forget about what we want to do and spend our time seeking to do what He wants us to do? Are we willing to give up what the world calls the good life for what Scripture calls the godly life?

> [37] "Anyone who loves his father or mother more than me is not worthy of me; anyone who loves his son or daughter more than me is not worthy of me; [38] and anyone who does not take his cross and follow me is not worthy of me. [39] Whoever finds his life will lose it, and whoever loses his life for my sake will find it. (Matthew 10:37-39).

> [7] Have nothing to do with godless myths and old wives' tales; rather, train yourself to be godly. (1Timothy 4:7).

If we love Christ why do we love Him? Scripture tells us why.

> [10] This is love: not that we loved God, but that he loved us... (1John 4:10).

> [19] We love because he first loved us. (1John 4:19).

Will Christ continue to love us? Let us see what He says.

> [10] If you obey my commands, you will remain in my love, just as I have obeyed my Father's commands and remain in his love. (John 15:10).

> [27] My sheep listen to my voice; I know them, and they follow me. [28] I give them eternal life, and they shall never perish; no one can snatch them out of my hand. (John 10:27-28).

Christ is to be the love of your life and the focus of your life. Scripture is clear: Whether or not you love Christ will be shown by whether or not you obey Him. As you examine yourself ask the question: Do I know what Christ commands? Do I obey His commands? If I don't know what Christ commands, whose fault is that? What am I going to do about it? If I don't obey Christ's commands, who is at fault? What am I going to do about it?

5. Have I "counted the cost" of being a Christian? This relates to obedience. Salvation is a free gift to us — Christ paid the price for our sins, and we are saved by God's grace. Living the Christian life is a whole different story. It's hard work. It's a struggle with sin, trials, and temptations. It's a tug of war between doing our will and doing God's will. It's being persecuted. It's suffering. We probably will not be persecuted or suffer unto death as the Apostles did. Perhaps we will not face the degree of persecution and suffering that many Christians do in foreign countries. Nonetheless, Christians in this country do experience persecution

and suffering. Furthermore, persecution of Christians appears to be on the increase, and I believe it will become more severe in the days ahead.

[12] **In fact, everyone who wants to live a godly life in Christ Jesus will be persecuted...** (2 Timothy 3:12).

[3] **Not only so, but we also rejoice in our sufferings, because we know that suffering produces perseverance;** [4] **perseverance, character; and character, hope.** (Romans 5:3-4).

[17] **Now if we are children, then we are heirs—heirs of God and co-heirs with Christ, if indeed we share in his sufferings in order that we may also share in his glory.** (Romans 8:17).

[25] **Large crowds were traveling with Jesus, and turning to them he said:** [26] **"If anyone comes to me and does not hate his father and mother, his wife and children, his brothers and sisters—yes, even his own life—he cannot be my disciple.** [27] **And anyone who does not carry his cross and follow me cannot be my disciple.** [28] **"Suppose one of you wants to build a tower. Will he not first sit down and estimate the cost to see if he has enough money to complete it?** [29] **For if he lays the foundation and is not able to finish it, everyone who sees it will ridicule him,** [30] **saying, 'This fellow began to build and was not able to finish.'** [31] **"Or suppose a king is about to go to war against another king. Will he not first sit down and consider whether he is able with ten thousand men to oppose the one coming against him with twenty thousand?** [32] **If he is not able, he will send a delegation while the other is still a long way off and will ask for terms of peace.** [33] **In the same way, any of you who does not give up everything he has cannot be my disciple.** (Luke 14:25-33).

It costs to follow Christ. It costs all that we have. Is this the way we are living? We should live so that men see Christ in us and God sees us in Christ. If we do, it will cost us. We will lose our life here on earth, but we will gain a life in heaven.

J. C. Ryle was a minister in England during the 19th century. In his book <u>Expository Thoughts on Luke</u> he referrers to our last Scripture passage (Luke 14:25-33). Ryle has this to say:

> *"We learn, secondly, from this passage, that those who are thinking of following Christ should be warned to "count the cost." This is a lesson which was intended for the multitudes who followed our Lord without thought and consideration, and was enforced by examples drawn from building and from war. It is a lesson which will be found useful in every age of the church.*
>
> *It costs something to be a true Christian. Let that never be forgotten. To be a mere nominal Christian, and go to Church, is cheap and easy work. But to hear Christ's voice, and follow Christ, and believe in Christ, and confess Christ, requires much self-denial. It will cost us our sins, and our self-righteousness, and our ease, and our worldliness. All — all must be given up. We must fight an enemy, who comes against us with twenty thousand followers. We must build a tower in troublous times. Our Lord Jesus Christ would have us thoroughly understand this. He bids us "count the cost."*
>
> *"Well would it be for the Church and the world if the ministers of Christ would always remember their Master's conduct in this passage. Often, — far too often, — people are built up in self-deception, and encouraged to think they are converted when in reality they are not converted at all. Feelings are supposed to be faith. Convictions are supposed to be grace. These things ought not so to be. By all means let us encourage the first beginnings of religion in a soul. But never let us urge people forward without telling them what true Christianity entails. Never let us hide from them the battle and the toil. Let us say to them "come with us," — but let us also say, "count the cost."*

Scripture is clear, what God requires of the Christian is complete submission, total surrender, and perfect obedience. Because we are sinners, we are not able to meet God's requirement. However, we are not excused from trying our very best. If we are rationalizing away our disobedience instead of trying our best to obey God, we had better repent. God knows our thoughts and our hearts. He will hold us accountable. <u>Whatever excuses or reasons we give for not doing our best to obey God is our way of saying "the cost is too high."</u> We want to "have our cake and eat it too." We want to be a Christian without having to do all that God commands. We are willing to do some things for God, but we want to run our own lives. Christ says in Luke 14:25-33 that we must be willing to give up everything or we cannot be His disciple. Not being His disciple means we don't belong to Him — we are not Christians — we are not saved. Christ is not telling us this is how to be saved. He is making it clear that if we are saved, then this will be the attitude of our hearts. Christ is not calling Christians to give up all that they have; He is calling Christians to have hearts that are <u>willing</u> to give up all that they have. However, He is calling Christians to <u>actually</u> give up all that He asks of them. Don't think of this as just money and material goods. It is also our time, our energy, our relationships, our careers, where we live, and how well we live. He may call us to the mission field. Tradition says that all the Apostles were martyred except for the Apostle John. Are you willing to die for Christ? Have you "counted the cost" of being a Christian? Does the cost seem too high?

Have you "counted the cost" of not being a Christian?

[15] **If anyone's name was not found written in the book of life, he was thrown into the lake of fire.** (Revelation 20:15).

[1] **We must pay more careful attention, therefore, to what we have heard, so that we do not drift away.** [2] **For if the message spoken by angels was binding,**

and every violation and disobedience received its just punishment, [3] how shall we escape if we ignore such a great salvation? (Hebrews 2:1-3a).

6. Do I exhibit the fruit of the Spirit? When we examine ourselves we should check to see if our lives show forth the fruit of the Spirit.

[22] But the fruit of the Spirit is love, joy, peace, patience, kindness, goodness, faithfulness [23] gentleness and self-control. (Galatians 5:22-23a).

The fruit of the Spirit is work done in the Christian by the Spirit. This fruit will be covered in detail later in this book. Examine yourself by checking each characteristic of the fruit one at a time to see how you stand. Keep in mind that the question is not: Can I make myself act this way? The question is: Am I this way? Is something happening in me to cause me to be more this way? Is the Holy Spirit producing this fruit in me?

7. Does God's Spirit testify to me that I am a Christian?

[16] The Spirit himself testifies with our spirit that we are God's children. (Romans 8:16).

[24] Those who obey his commands live in him, and he in them. And this is how we know that he lives in us: We know it by the Spirit he gave us. (1 John 3:24).

Do you have promptings from the Holy Spirit that convince you that He indwells you — that you are a Christian? Another way the Spirit makes us aware that we are Christians is the internal war He wages with our sinful nature. When we find that we hate sin, don't want to sin, and fight against sin, then we can have confidence that it is the Spirit working in us.

¹⁶ So I say, live by the Spirit, and you will not gratify the desires of the sinful nature. ¹⁷ For the sinful nature desires what is contrary to the Spirit, and the Spirit what is contrary to the sinful nature. They are in conflict with each other, so that you do not do what you want. (Galatians 5:16-17)

8. Is the purpose of my life to glorify God? Have you considered that the purpose of your life is to glorify God? If so, do you live that way? Do you think about it daily and ask God what He would have you do to bring Him glory? Are you aware that God created everything?

¹⁶ For by him all things were created: things in heaven and on earth, visible and invisible, whether thrones or powers or rulers or authorities; all things were created by him and for him. (Colossians 1:16).

You are included in all that God created. God's purpose for His creation is to glorify Himself.

⁹ All the nations you have made will come and worship before you, O Lord; they will bring glory to your name. (Psalm 86:9).

⁵ May the God who gives endurance and encouragement give you a spirit of unity among yourselves as you follow Christ Jesus, ⁶ so that with one heart and mouth you may glorify the God and Father of our Lord Jesus Christ. (Romans 15:5-6).

¹⁹ Jesus said this to indicate the kind of death by which Peter would glorify God. Then he said to him, "Follow me!" (John 21:19).

⁸ This is to my Father's glory, that you bear much fruit, showing yourselves to be my disciples. (John 15:8).

If to glorify God is not the purpose of your life, what is the purpose of your life? The purpose of the Christian life is to glorify God.

9. Am I doing the work that God called me to do?

> [10] **For we are God's workmanship, created in Christ Jesus to do good works, which God prepared in advance for us to do.** (Ephesians 2:10).

Before the world was made God determined what He wanted each Christian to do. Were you aware of this before now? If so, have you been doing your best to do what He has called you to do? Every Christian is called to study the Bible, to pray, to witness, and to help the poor and needy. These are just a few of the things we are called to do. Are you doing these? Are you trying to learn more about what in particular you are called to do so that you can do it?

10. Do I love fellow Christians?

> [11] **Dear friends, since God so loved us, we also ought to love one another. [12] No one has ever seen God; but if we love one another, God lives in us and his love is made complete in us.** (1John 4:11-12).

> [19] **We love because he first loved us. [20] If anyone says, "I love God," yet hates his brother, he is a liar. For anyone who does not love his brother, whom he has seen, cannot love God, whom he has not seen. [21] And he has given us this command: Whoever loves God must also love his brother.** (1John 4:19-21).

Christians have a spiritual bond with Christ, and through Christ they have a spiritual bond with each other. We are all members of the body of Christ. As such, we should certainly love each other. God loves His children, and we should love those who God loves. Are you fellowshipping with other Christians? Are you showing them love?

SALVATION

Earlier I said that there are probably some readers who think they are Christians but who are not. I also said that this was my case until, at age 41, I learned that I was not a Christian. However, I also was told what God's Word said about how to be saved. At that time I became a Christian — I was saved. My testimony is on page 161 of this book. Some readers who have found from their self examination that they are not Christians may wonder how you become one. We will address that, but first I want to ask the reader a question.

If you died at this moment would you go to heaven? There are three logical answers: the first is "no," the second is "I am not sure," and the third is "yes." The second answer of "I'm not sure" also covers thoughts such as "I think so" or "I hope so." All of these indicate an uncertainty. Knowing that you are going to heaven when you die is called assurance of your salvation. Of course, there is such a thing as a false assurance. There are people who are not Christians, but they think they are; therefore, they have a false assurance. There are also people of non-Christian religions that have a false assurance. They see themselves as deserving heaven or earning heaven. In addition, there are a number of people who hold to universalism, which teaches that everyone goes to heaven regardless of what you do or what you believe. Therefore, they too have a false assurance. However, God wants those who <u>are</u> going to heaven to <u>know</u> that they are going there. He makes this clear in His Bible.

Again, this raises the question of the Bible. Do you believe it is God's Word? Do you believe what the Bible teaches is the truth? Jesus Christ tells us that it is.

> [17] Sanctify them by the truth; your word is truth. (John 17:17).

> [4] Jesus answered, "It is written: 'Man does not live on bread alone, but on every word that comes from the mouth of God.'" (Matthew 4:4).

What we call the Old Testament was the only Scripture that Jesus and His Apostles had. We can think of it as their Bible. The New Testament was not yet written. They believed their Bible and quoted it in their writings. Some of the Apostles along with other believers wrote about Jesus Christ. They knew Him as their Savior and Lord who died for their sins, was resurrected, and ascended to Heaven. They knew this to be the truth and were willing to die for it. Their letters and writings were written to build and strengthen the church. Accurate copies of these letters and writings were made and passed down through the church and some of them later became our New Testament.

The Apostle Paul (who was formally known as Saul) was, at one time, a strong persecutor of the church.

> [54] When they heard this, they were furious and gnashed their teeth at him. [55] But Stephen, full of the Holy Spirit, looked up to heaven and saw the glory of God, and Jesus standing at the right hand of God. [56] "Look," he said, "I see heaven open and the Son of Man standing at the right hand of God." [57] At this they covered their ears and, yelling at the top of their voices, they all rushed at him, [58] dragged him out of the city and began to stone him. Meanwhile, the witnesses laid their clothes at the feet of a young man named Saul. [59] While they were stoning him, Stephen prayed, "Lord Jesus, receive my spirit." [60] Then he fell on his knees and cried out, "Lord, do not hold this sin against them." When he had said this, he fell asleep. (Acts 7:54-60).

[1] And Saul was there, giving approval to his death. On that day a great persecution broke out against the church at Jerusalem, and all except the apostles were scattered throughout Judea and Samaria. [2] Godly men buried Stephen and mourned deeply for him. [3] But Saul began to destroy the church. Going from house to house, he dragged off men and women and put them in prison. (Acts 8:1-3).

Christ appeared to Paul on the Road to Damascus and Paul was converted. The Pharisee Saul, later known as Paul, was saved, and now he who had been such an enemy of God became a wonderful servant of God. Paul is the author of 13 of the 27 books in the New Testament.

[1] Meanwhile, Saul was still breathing out murderous threats against the Lord's disciples. He went to the high priest [2] and asked him for letters to the synagogues in Damascus, so that if he found any there who belonged to the Way, whether men or women, he might take them as prisoners to Jerusalem. [3] As he neared Damascus on his journey, suddenly a light from heaven flashed around him. [4] He fell to the ground and heard a voice say to him, "Saul, Saul, why do you persecute me?" [5] "Who are you, Lord?" Saul asked. "I am Jesus, whom you are persecuting," he replied. [6] "Now get up and go into the city, and you will be told what you must do." [7] The men traveling with Saul stood there speechless; they heard the sound but did not see anyone. [8] Saul got up from the ground, but when he opened his eyes he could see nothing. So they led him by the hand into Damascus. [9] For three days he was blind, and did not eat or drink anything. [10] In Damascus there was a disciple named Ananias. The Lord called to him in a vision, "Ananias!" "Yes, Lord," he answered. [11] The Lord told him, "Go to the house of Judas on Straight Street and ask for a man from Tarsus named Saul, for he is praying. [12] In a vision he has seen a man named Ananias come and place his hands on him to restore his sight." [13] "Lord," Ananias answered, "I have heard many reports

about this man and all the harm he has done to your saints in Jerusalem. [14] And he has come here with authority from the chief priests to arrest all who call on your name." [15] But the Lord said to Ananias, "Go! This man is my chosen instrument to carry my name before the Gentiles and their kings and before the people of Israel. [16] I will show him how much he must suffer for my name." [17] Then Ananias went to the house and entered it. Placing his hands on Saul, he said, "Brother Saul, the Lord—Jesus, who appeared to you on the road as you were coming here—has sent me so that you may see again and be filled with the Holy Spirit." [18] Immediately, something like scales fell from Saul's eyes, and he could see again. He got up and was baptized, [19] and after taking some food, he regained his strength. Saul spent several days with the disciples in Damascus. (Acts 9:1-19).

Paul received the Gospel directly from the resurrected Jesus Christ and became an enthusiastic and hard working preacher and missionary.

[11] I want you to know, brothers, that the gospel I preached is not something that man made up. [12] I did not receive it from any man, nor was I taught it; rather, I received it by revelation from Jesus Christ. [13] For you have heard of my previous way of life in Judaism, how intensely I persecuted the church of God and tried to destroy it. [14] I was advancing in Judaism beyond many Jews of my own age and was extremely zealous for the traditions of my fathers. [15] But when God, who set me apart from birth and called me by his grace, was pleased [16] to reveal his Son in me so that I might preach him among the Gentiles, I did not consult any man, [17] nor did I go up to Jerusalem to see those who were apostles before I was, but I went immediately into Arabia and later returned to Damascus. [18] Then after three years, I went up to Jerusalem to get acquainted with Peter and stayed with him fifteen days. [19] I saw none of the other apostles—only James, the Lord's brother. [20] I assure you before God that what I am writing you is no lie. [21] Later I went to Syria and Cilicia. [22] I was

personally unknown to the churches of Judea that
are in Christ. [23] They only heard the report: "The man
who formerly persecuted us is now preaching the
faith he once tried to destroy." [24] And they praised
God because of me. (Galatians 1:11-24).

Paul suffered much in his Christian ministry, and
tradition indicates that Paul was beheaded outside of Rome.

[8] We do not want you to be uninformed, brothers,
about the hardships we suffered in the province of
Asia. We were under great pressure, far beyond our
ability to endure, so that we despaired even of life. [9]
Indeed, in our hearts we felt the sentence of death.
But this happened that we might not rely on
ourselves but on God, who raises the dead. [10] He has
delivered us from such a deadly peril, and he will
deliver us. On him we have set our hope that he will
continue to deliver us, [11] as you help us by your
prayers. Then many will give thanks on our behalf
for the gracious favor granted us in answer to the
prayers of many. (2 Corinthians 1:8-11).

[24] Five times I received from the Jews the forty
lashes minus one. [25] Three times I was beaten with
rods, once I was stoned, three times I was
shipwrecked, I spent a night and a day in the open
sea, [26] I have been constantly on the move. I have
been in danger from rivers, in danger from bandits,
in danger from my own countrymen, in danger from
Gentiles; in danger in the city, in danger in the
country, in danger at sea; and in danger from false
brothers. [27] I have labored and toiled and have often
gone without sleep; I have known hunger and thirst
and have often gone without food; I have been cold
and naked. [28] Besides everything else, I face daily
the pressure of my concern for all the churches.
(2 Corinthians 11:24-28).

[6] For I am already being poured out like a drink
offering, and the time has come for my departure. [7] I
have fought the good fight, I have finished the race, I

> have kept the faith. [8] Now there is in store for me the crown of righteousness, which the Lord, the righteous Judge, will award to me on that day—and not only to me, but also to all who have longed for his appearing. (2 Timothy 4:6-8).

Paul wrote about the large number of people who saw the resurrected Christ. At the time of his writing most of these were still living. We can imagine that some of them made a point of witnessing to the fact that Christ was resurrected.

> [1] Now, brothers, I want to remind you of the gospel I preached to you, which you received and on which you have taken your stand. [2] By this gospel you are saved, if you hold firmly to the word I preached to you. Otherwise, you have believed in vain. [3] For what I received I passed on to you as of first importance: that Christ died for our sins according to the Scriptures, [4] that he was buried, that he was raised on the third day according to the Scriptures, [5] and that he appeared to Peter, and then to the Twelve. [6] After that, he appeared to more than five hundred of the brothers at the same time, most of whom are still living, though some have fallen asleep. [7] Then he appeared to James, then to all the apostles, [8] and last of all he appeared to me also, as to one abnormally born. (1 Corinthians 15:1-8).

When Christ was condemned to die, the Apostle Judas who had betrayed Him became remorseful and killed himself. After the resurrection, the Apostles decided to choose someone to replace Judas. One requirement was that he must have seen the resurrected Christ.

> [21] Therefore it is necessary to choose one of the men who have been with us the whole time the Lord Jesus went in and out among us, [22] beginning from John's baptism to the time when Jesus was taken up from us. For one of these must become a witness with us of his resurrection." (Acts 1:21-22).

Peter said that the Apostles had seen the risen Christ.

³² God has raised this Jesus to life, and we are all witnesses of the fact. (Acts 2:32).

The Apostle John also tells us about seeing the resurrected Christ.

¹⁹ On the evening of that first day of the week, when the disciples were together, with the doors locked for fear of the Jews, Jesus came and stood among them and said, "Peace be with you!" ²⁰ After he said this, he showed them his hands and side. The disciples were overjoyed when they saw the Lord. (John 20:19-20).

²⁴ Now Thomas (called Didymus), one of the Twelve, was not with the disciples when Jesus came. ²⁵ So the other disciples told him, "We have seen the Lord!" But he said to them, "Unless I see the nail marks in his hands and put my finger where the nails were, and put my hand into his side, I will not believe it." ²⁶ A week later his disciples were in the house again, and Thomas was with them. Though the doors were locked, Jesus came and stood among them and said, "Peace be with you!" ²⁷ Then he said to Thomas, "Put your finger here; see my hands. Reach out your hand and put it into my side. Stop doubting and believe." ²⁸ Thomas said to him, "My Lord and my God!" ²⁹ Then Jesus told him, "Because you have seen me, you have believed; blessed are those who have not seen and yet have believed." (John 20:24-29).

By faith we believe the Bible. However, there are a number of things that give credence to our faith. One of the most compelling is the writers of the New Testament who saw the risen Christ or talked with people who saw Him. In fact, Jesus had brothers who did not believe in Him until after the Resurrection. (See Matthew 13:55, 1 Corinthians 9:5, Galatians 1:19 and Jude 1) Scholars are convinced that two of those brothers wrote two of the books of the New Testament, James and Jude. This was not a group of liars, and it was not a group of crazy people. Do we have any reason to doubt that the Apostles, Christ's brothers, and others were witnesses to the fact that Jesus lived, died, and was resurrected? History tells us that after the Resurrection Christ's brother, James, became the head of the church at Jerusalem. He also wrote and spoke of Christ. These were men of integrity who related what they saw and what others who were eyewitnesses saw. In doing so they put their own lives in jeopardy. We have every reason to believe them. They wrote about what they knew to be true.

Do you believe that George Washington and Abraham Lincoln lived? How about Alexander The Great or Hannibal, who took his army, which included elephants, across the Alps? What about various rulers of different countries that lived hundreds of years ago? What you know and what you believe about these men is based on what you have read or heard. Then how could you not believe the writers of the New Testament and what they say about Jesus Christ? They were there.

> [32] **God has raised this Jesus to life, and we are all witnesses of the fact.** (Acts 2:32).

> [1] **That which was from the beginning, which we have heard, which we have seen with our eyes, which we have looked at and our hands have touched—this we proclaim concerning the Word of life.** [2] **The life appeared; we have seen it and testify to it, and we proclaim to you the eternal life, which was with the Father and has appeared to us.** [3] **We proclaim to you what we have seen and heard, so that you also may have fellowship with us. And our fellowship is with the Father and with his Son, Jesus Christ.**
> (1 John 1:1-3).

> [3] **For what I received I passed on to you as of first importance: that Christ died for our sins according to the Scriptures,** [4] **that he was buried, that he was raised on the third day according to the Scriptures,** [5] **and that he appeared to Peter, and then to the**

Twelve. **⁶ After that, he appeared to more than five hundred of the brothers at the same time, most of whom are still living, though some have fallen asleep. ⁷ Then he appeared to James, then to all the apostles...** (1 Corinthians 15:3-7).

¹⁶ We did not follow cleverly invented stories when we told you about the power and coming of our Lord Jesus Christ, but we were eyewitnesses of his majesty. (2 Peter 1:16).

If you say you don't believe the Bible, you have sinned. In essence you are calling God a liar. Paul tells us this is God's Word (He used men to write it) and it is written for our benefit. We are to believe what it says and practice what it teaches.

¹⁶ All Scripture is God-breathed and is useful for teaching, rebuking, correcting and training in righteousness, ¹⁷ so that the man of God may be thoroughly equipped for every good work.
(2 Timothy 3:16-17).

If you have a problem believing the Bible, be aware that there are three enemies that will fight to keep you from believing it. These are the same enemies that Christians have, and they will attempt to get Christians to doubt the Bible. These three are the world, the flesh, and the devil.

The world lures, entices, and tempts us to enjoy its pleasures. It offers sin in place of salvation.

¹⁵ Do not love the world or anything in the world. If anyone loves the world, the love of the Father is not in him. ¹⁶ For everything in the world—the cravings of sinful man, the lust of his eyes and the boasting of what he has and does—comes not from the Father but from the world. ¹⁷ The world and its desires pass away, but the man who does the will of God lives forever. (1 John 2:15-17).

> [4] You adulterous people, don't you know that friendship with the world is hatred toward God? Anyone who chooses to be a friend of the world becomes an enemy of God. (James 4:4).

The flesh, which is our sinful human nature, rebels against God. It suppresses the truth about God. It is hostile toward God. It cannot please God. The flesh is an internal enemy, a traitor within us.

> [18] The wrath of God is being revealed from heaven against all the godlessness and wickedness of men who suppress the truth by their wickedness... (Romans 1:1).

> [18] I know that nothing good lives in me, that is, in my sinful nature. (Romans 7:18a).

> [7] the sinful mind is hostile to God... (Romans 8:7).

> [8] Those controlled by the sinful nature cannot please God. (Romans 8:8).

The third enemy, Satan, (also called the evil one) is very powerful. However, he is not all-knowing, or present everywhere at one time as some people think. But, he does have a large number of demons helping him. Even among those that believe the Bible, there is a tendency to either forget or underestimate the powerful influence Satan has had on mankind and continues to have today. You could be influenced by Satan in your unbelief. Remember how he questioned what God had said as he was tempting Eve to sin, and through Eve he was tempting Adam.

> [1] Now the serpent was more crafty than any of the wild animals the LORD God had made. He said to the woman, "Did God really say, 'You must not eat from any tree in the garden'?" [2] The woman said to the serpent, "We may eat fruit from the trees in the garden, [3] but God did say, 'You must not eat fruit from the tree that is in the middle of the garden, and

you must not touch it, or you will die.'" [4] "You will
not surely die," the serpent said to the woman. [5] "For
God knows that when you eat of it your eyes will be
opened, and you will be like God, knowing good and
evil." [6] When the woman saw that the fruit of the tree
was good for food and pleasing to the eye, and also
desirable for gaining wisdom, she took some and ate
it. She also gave some to her husband, who was
with her, and he ate it. (Genesis 3:1-6).

Satan keeps people from coming to Christ.

[19] When anyone hears the message about the
kingdom and does not understand it, the evil one
comes and snatches away what was sown in his
heart... (Matthew 13:19).

If you don't believe the Bible, where would you find out
who God is and what He is like? Creation tells us that there
is a God, but the Bible tells us who that God is, what He
does, and what He expects of us.

If you only believe some of the Bible, are you not
putting yourself on a par with God? You are indicating that
you are intelligent enough to know what God has said and
what He has not said. You are also calling God a liar when
you don't believe certain parts of the Bible. Is that not only
dangerous to do, but also arrogant on your part? God says
He wrote it.

If you do not believe any of the Bible, but you believe
there is a God, then you are in a position of not knowing
anything about God. You only know that there is a God.
Your god becomes who you want him to be. He is a god of
your imagination — he is whoever and whatever you want
him to be. And, he will require of you only what you are
willing for him to require. You are not alone if you think this
way. The Bible warns man against thinking he knows what is
best.

[7] Do not be wise in your own eyes; fear the LORD and
shun evil. (Proverbs 3:7).

The Bible further tells us to look to God and not ourselves to understand things.

> [5] Trust in the LORD with all your heart and lean not on your own understanding... (Proverbs 3:5).

There are other reasons for believing the Bible is God's Word and that it is the absolute truth. However, we will not go into them here other than to point out that the Bible claims to be written by God.

> [20] Above all, you must understand that no prophecy of Scripture came about by the prophet's own interpretation. [21] For prophecy never had its origin in the will of man, but men spoke from God as they were carried along by the Holy Spirit.
> (2 Peter 1:20-21).

> [13] And we also thank God continually because, when you received the word of God, which you heard from us, you accepted it not as the word of men, but as it actually is, the word of God, which is at work in you who believe. (1 Thessalonians 2:13).

If you do not believe the Bible, then you may believe one of the many religions that were started by man. These false religions originate and are authored in a relatively short period of time by a single person. They do not have a savior, and if they offer any hope of heaven it usually is based on how well you follow their rules. In some cases, they utilize the Bible or verses from the Bible along with the writings of the founder of the religion. They may even include Jesus in their religion, but not as Savior. They will call Him a good man or a prophet, but they will not acknowledge Him for who He really is.

Compare this with Christianity: God wrote the Bible over a period of approximately 1,500 years. He used over 40 different men as His instruments in writing it. God the Son came down from heaven and was born as a human being. He walked on this earth as fully man and fully God. He is the Savior of those who put their trust in Him.

[1] In the beginning was the Word, and the Word was with God, and the Word was God. [2] He was with God in the beginning. (John 1:1-2).

[14] The Word became flesh and made his dwelling among us. We have seen his glory, the glory of the One and Only, who came from the Father, full of grace and truth. (John 1:14).

[5] But you know that he appeared so that he might take away our sins. And in him is no sin. (1 John 3:5).

[6] Who, being in very nature God, did not consider equality with God something to be grasped, [7] but made himself nothing, taking the very nature of a servant, being made in human likeness. [8] And being found in appearance as a man, he humbled himself and became obedient to death—even death on a cross! (Philippians 2:6-8).

Now let us see what God's Word says about how to be saved. The Bible teaches that we are all sinners. In fact, because of Adam's first sin, we all come into this world with a sinful nature. When Adam sinned, we all sinned as it were.

[12] Therefore, just as sin entered the world through one man, and death through sin, and in this way death came to all men, because all sinned... (Romans 5:12).

Adam was our Federal Head, and his first sin is referred to as "original sin." From that time on, all men are born with a sinful nature.

[5] Surely I was sinful at birth, sinful from the time my mother conceived me. (Psalm 51:5).

We are not sinners because we sin, but we sin because we are sinners. We follow the desires of our sinful natures.

> [1] As for you, you were dead in your transgressions and sins, [2] in which you used to live when you followed the ways of this world and of the ruler of the kingdom of the air, the spirit who is now at work in those who are disobedient. [3] All of us also lived among them at one time, gratifying the cravings of our sinful nature and following its desires and thoughts. Like the rest, we were by nature objects of wrath. (Ephesians 2:1-3).

Any who claim to be without sin deceive themselves.

> [8] If we claim to be without sin, we deceive ourselves and the truth is not in us. (1 John 1:8).

> [20] There is not a righteous man on earth who does what is right and never sins. (Ecclesiastes 7:20).

> [9] Who can say, "I have kept my heart pure; I am clean and without sin"? (Proverbs 20:9).

> [23] for all have sinned and fall short of the glory of God... (Romans 3:23).

Sin separates us from God. This separation is spiritual death.

> [23] For the wages of sin is death, but the gift of God is eternal life in Christ Jesus our Lord. (Romans 6:23).

> [6] The mind of sinful man is death, but the mind controlled by the Spirit is life and peace...
> (Romans 8:6).

> [18] They are darkened in their understanding and separated from the life of God because of the ignorance that is in them due to the hardening of their hearts. (Ephesians 4:18).

There is a penalty to be paid for sin.

> [8] He will punish those who do not know God and do not obey the gospel of our Lord Jesus. [9] They will be punished with everlasting destruction and shut out

from the presence of the Lord and from the majesty of his power. (2 Thessalonians 1:8-9).

[41] The Son of Man will send out his angels, and they will weed out of his kingdom everything that causes sin and all who do evil. [42] They will throw them into the fiery furnace, where there will be weeping and gnashing of teeth. (Matthew 13:41-42).

When we are saved, our salvation saves us from the awful penalty of sin — the penalty of spending eternity in hell. We may undergo the natural consequences of our sins here on earth. Also, God may chasten us for them in this life, but we will not have to pay for them in the hereafter.

Christ came to live a sinless life, to live a life of obedience to God's law, and to fulfill the prophecies about His life, death, and resurrection.

[17] "Do not think that I have come to abolish the Law or the Prophets; I have not come to abolish them but to fulfill them. (Matthew 5:17).

Christ took the punishment for our sins upon Himself. He paid for all our past, present, and future sins.

[24] He himself bore our sins in his body on the tree, so that we might die to sins and live for righteousness; by his wounds you have been healed. (1 Peter 2:24).

[21] God made him who had no sin to be sin for us, so that in him we might become the righteousness of God. (2 Corinthians 5:21).

[18] For Christ died for sins once for all, the righteous for the unrighteous, to bring you to God. He was put to death in the body but made alive by the Spirit... (1 Peter 3:18).

After Christ died for our sins, He was raised from the dead. God raised Him from the dead to confirm that His work was complete and successful. It also confirmed that Christ was who He claimed to be.

> [31] **For he has set a day when he will judge the world with justice by the man he has appointed. He has given proof of this to all men by raising him from the dead."** (Acts 17:31).

At the close of His Resurrection appearances Christ was taken up to heaven.

> [50] **When he had led them out to the vicinity of Bethany, he lifted up his hands and blessed them.** [51] **While he was blessing them, he left them and was taken up into heaven.** [52] **Then they worshiped him and returned to Jerusalem with great joy.** [53] **And they stayed continually at the temple, praising God.** (Luke 24:50-53).

Let us review what we have been discussing. We see that prior to salvation, we are sinners who are in bondage to sin and we are headed for hell. We also see that Christ came, lived a sinless life, and died on the cross to pay the penalty for our sins. God has shown His approval and acceptance of Christ's sacrifice by resurrecting Him and seating Him at His right hand.

In view of these facts, what must we do if we are to spend eternity in heaven with Christ? We will address that question, but first let me point out the wrong way that so very many people are pursuing salvation. It is by trying to do good or by going to the right church or belonging to the right denomination. They are in error; they are deceived by Satan, and they are on the road to hell. Unless they discover the truth and change roads, hell will be their destination. Christ tells us the road to heaven is narrow and only a few travel it.

> [13] **"Enter through the narrow gate. For wide is the gate and broad is the road that leads to destruction, and many enter through it.** [14] **But small is the gate and narrow the road that leads to life, and only a few find it.** (Matthew 7:13-14).

Most of the people on the road to hell are trying to work their way to heaven. They are trying to earn God's favor.

They are working to please God and show that they deserve
to go to heaven. They think they can impress God with the
moral life they are leading and the good deeds they do.
However, God's Word tells us that the deeds of the unsaved
man are like filthy rags to God.

> [6] **All of us have become like one who is unclean, and
> all our righteous acts are like filthy rags; we all
> shrivel up like a leaf, and like the wind our sins
> sweep us away.** (Isaiah 64:6).

Working your way to heaven is a man-made religion. It has
great appeal because man gets credit for doing something.
However, as stated above, it does not lead to heaven. It
leads to hell.

> [25] **There is a way that seems right to a man, but in the
> end it leads to death.** (Proverbs 16:25).

Christ was the only sinless man — He kept the law perfectly.
Man is a sinner and has broken the law many times. Even if
we had committed only one sin, it would be the same as
breaking all of the law.

> [10] **For whoever keeps the whole law and yet stumbles
> at just one point is guilty of breaking all of it.**
> (James 2:10).

As sinners who have sinned and broken the law, why would
we ever think that we could earn heaven by trying to keep
the law? The Bible makes it clear that we cannot.

> [20] **Therefore no one will be declared righteous in his
> sight by observing the law; rather, through the law
> we become conscious of sin.** (Romans 3:20).

> [10] **All who rely on observing the law are under a
> curse, for it is written: "Cursed is everyone who
> does not continue to do everything written in the
> Book of the Law."** (Galatians 3:10).

> [16] know that a man is not justified by observing the law, but by faith in Jesus Christ. So we, too, have put our faith in Christ Jesus that we may be justified by faith in Christ and not by observing the law, because by observing the law no one will be justified. (Galatians 2:16).

> [4] You who are trying to be justified by law have been alienated from Christ; you have fallen away from grace. (Galatians 5:4).

If we are to be saved, the Bible tells us we must believe in Jesus Christ. In fact, the Bible tells us that it is only through Christ that we can get to heaven.

> [6] Jesus answered, "I am the way and the truth and the life. No one comes to the Father except through me. (John 14:6).

> [12] Salvation is found in no one else, for there is no other name under heaven given to men by which we must be saved." (Acts 4:12).

What does the Bible mean when it says believe in Jesus Christ? It means much more than most people think it does. It is not only an intellectual accent but of utmost importance it is a heartfelt trust. It means to not only believe the facts about Him, but also to turn to Him and acknowledge that you are a sinner, lost in your sins, and headed to hell. And then repent of (turn from) your sins and ask Him to please forgive you and to come into your life and be your Savior and Lord. Believing in Him means you not only believe He is the Savior and can save you, but you actually put yourself in His hands. You trust Him to save you, and you trust Him alone — nothing else. Those who in faith turn to Christ in this manner will go to heaven. Those who do not will go to hell. This is not man's opinion — it is what God says in His Bible.

[16] "For God so loved the world that he gave his one and only Son, that whoever believes in him shall not perish but have eternal life. [17] For God did not send his Son into the world to condemn the world, but to save the world through him. [18] Whoever believes in him is not condemned, but whoever does not believe stands condemned already because he has not believed in the name of God's one and only Son. (John 3:16-18).

[35] The Father loves the Son and has placed everything in his hands. [36] Whoever believes in the Son has eternal life, but whoever rejects the Son will not see life, for God's wrath remains on him." (John 3:35-36).

[23] But he continued, "You are from below; I am from above. You are of this world; I am not of this world. [24] I told you that you would die in your sins; if you do not believe that I am the one I claim to be, you will indeed die in your sins." (John 8:23-24).

If you agree with what the Bible teaches, I ask you this question: Have you repented of your sins and trusted Christ to forgive you and be your Savior? If you have not, let me encourage you to do so right now. Dear Reader, turn to God and be saved for it is God's wish that all men would be saved, and that includes you.

[3] This is good, and pleases God our Savior, [4] who wants all men to be saved and to come to a knowledge of the truth. (1 Timothy 2:3-4).

In sincerity, believing that Christ can save you and will save you, pray the following prayer:

Dear God, I confess that I am a sinner. I am lost in my sins. Please have mercy on me. I thank you that your Son, Jesus Christ, died for my sins. I ask Him to come into my life to be my Lord and Savior, to forgive my sins, and to do with my life as He pleases. I thank you that as I pray, this is done. In Jesus' name I pray.

God wants you to know that you are saved. If you prayed in sincerity, believing that Christ could and would save you, then be assured that you are saved according to God Himself.

> [9] The Lord is not slow in keeping his promise, as some understand slowness. He is patient with you, not wanting anyone to perish, but everyone to come to repentance. (2 Peter 3:9).

> [16] "For God so loved the world that he gave his one and only Son, that whoever believes in him shall not perish but have eternal life. (John 3:16).

> [11] And this is the testimony: God has given us eternal life, and this life is in his Son. [12] He who has the Son has life; he who does not have the Son of God does not have life. [13] I write these things to you who believe in the name of the Son of God so that you may know that you have eternal life.
> (1 John 5:11-13).

Dear Reader, if you have just been saved, realize that it is God who has done it all. It is by God's grace. He chose you to be saved. He regenerated you (gave you spiritual life) so that you could understand and believe the Gospel. He even worked in you to cause you to turn to Christ for salvation.

> [13] But we ought always to thank God for you, brothers loved by the Lord, because from the beginning God chose you to be saved through the sanctifying work of the Spirit and through belief in the truth. (2 Thessalonians 2:13).

> [13...] for it is God who works in you to will and to act according to his good purpose. (Philippians 2:13).

God gave you the faith with which you trusted Christ to save you.

> [8] For it is by grace you have been saved, through faith—and this not from yourselves, it is the gift of God—[9] not by works, so that no one can boast. (Ephesians 2:8-9).

We have seen that you cannot be saved by doing good works (deeds). However, once you are saved you are to do good works. Ask God to show you what He wants you to do. However, even though we should be diligent to do good works, let us not be mistaken: good works did not save us, and we do not keep ourselves saved by our works. God saved us and God keeps us saved. Those that God saves can never be lost. You cannot lose your salvation.

> [27] **My sheep listen to my voice; I know them, and they follow me.** [28] **I give them eternal life, and they shall never perish; no one can snatch them out of my hand.** [29] **My Father, who has given them to me, is greater than all; no one can snatch them out of my Father's hand.** [30] **I and the Father are one."**
> (John 10:27-30).

Why did God save you? He saved you because it pleased Him to do so. It was nothing about you that caused Him to save you. It is the same with whomever God saves. It just pleases Him to save us. It fits His plan and purpose. God saves His elect whom He chose before the creation of the world.

> [1] **Paul, an apostle of Christ Jesus by the will of God, To the saints in Ephesus, the faithful in Christ Jesus:** [2] **Grace and peace to you from God our Father and the Lord Jesus Christ.** [3] **Praise be to the God and Father of our Lord Jesus Christ, who has blessed us in the heavenly realms with every spiritual blessing in Christ.** [4] **For he chose us in him before the creation of the world to be holy and blameless in his sight. In love** [5] **he predestined us to be adopted as his sons through Jesus Christ, in accordance with his pleasure and will...**
> (Ephesians 1:1-5).

The doctrine of election is a difficult doctrine for many people. However, it is taught in the Bible. Once we make a study of it and begin to understand something about it, we find it is very humbling. One does not have to believe the doctrine of election to be saved. However, most people who do believe it find that their walk with God is strengthened.

The "elect" are the same as the "called" or the "chosen." The "elect" are people that God has decreed will be saved. Moreover, they are the only ones who will be saved. Both <u>The Baptist Confession of Faith</u> of 1689 and the <u>Westminster Confession of Faith,</u> among other Confessions, make clear that the Bible teaches election.

<u>The Baptist Confession of Faith</u> chpt. 11, pgh. 4

> *4. God did from all eternity decree to justify all the elect, and Christ did in the fullness of time die for their sins, and rise again for their justification; nevertheless, they are not justified personally, until the Holy Spirit doth in due time actually apply Christ unto them.*
> Gal. 3:8. 1 Pet. 1:2. 1 Tim. 2:6. Rom. 4:25. Col. 1:21,22. Tit. 3:4-7.

<u>The Baptist Confession of Faith</u> chpt. 3, pgh. 6

> *6. As God hath appointed the elect unto glory, so he hath, by the eternal and most free purpose of his will, foreordained all the means thereunto; where they who are elected, being fallen in Adam, are redeemed by Christ, are effectually called unto faith in Christ, by his Spirit working in due season, are justified, adopted, sanctified, and kept by his power through faith unto salvation; neither are any other redeemed by Christ, or effectually called, justified, adopted, sanctified, and saved but the elect only.*
> 1 Pet. 1:2. 2 Thess. 2:13. 1 Thess. 5:9,10. Rom. 8:30. 2 Thess. 2:13. 1 Pet. 1:5. John 10:26; 17:9; 6:64.

<u>The Westminster Confession of Faith</u> chp. 10, pgh 1

1. All those whom God hath predestinated unto life, and those only, He is pleased, in His appointed and accepted time, effectually to call, by His Word and Spirit, out of that state of sin and death, in which they are by nature, to grace and salvation, by Jesus Christ; enlightening their minds spiritually and savingly to understand the things of God, taking away their heart of stone, and giving unto them an heart of flesh; renewing their wills, and, by His almighty power, determining them to that which is good, and effectually drawing them to Jesus Christ: yet so, as they come most freely, being made willing by His grace.
Rom. 8:30. Rom. 11:7. Eph. 1:10,11. 2 Thes. 2:13,14. 2 Cor. 3:3,6. Rom. 8:2. Eph. 2:1-6. 2 Tim. 1:9,10. Acts 26:18. 1 Cor. 2:10,12. Eph 1:17,18. Ezk. 36:26. Ezk. 11:19. Phil. 2:13. Deut. 30:6. Ezk. 36.27. Eph. 1:19. Jh. 6:44,45. Ps. 110:3, Jh. 6:37. Rom. 6:16, 17,18.

In the <u>Articles of Religion of the Episcopal Church in the United States of America</u>, the 17th Article states the following pertaining to Predestination and Election:

Predestination to life is the everlasting purpose of God, whereby (before the foundations of the world were laid) he hath constantly decreed by his counsel secret to us, to deliver from curse and damnation those whom he hath chosen in Christ out of mankind, and to bring them by Christ to everlasting salvation, as vessels made to honor. Wherefore they which he endued with so excellent a benefit of God be called according to God's purpose by his Spirit working in due season: they through grace obey the calling: they be justified freely: they be made sons of

God by adoption: they be made like the image of his only-begotten Son Jesus Christ: they walk religiously in good works, and at length, by God's mercy, they attain to everlasting felicity.

A statement similar to the one above is made in the Thirty-nine Articles of the Church of England.

The teaching of predestination and election is not a teaching of any one denomination. It is like the teaching of salvation or God's sovereignty — it is the teaching of the Bible. And, like the teaching of salvation and God's sovereignty, it is being ignored more and more as time passes. People want to hear a watered-down message that makes them feel comfortable. They don't want to hear the truth of God's Word.

> [3] For the time will come when men will not put up with sound doctrine. Instead, to suit their own desires, they will gather around them a great number of teachers to say what their itching ears want to hear. [4] They will turn their ears away from the truth and turn aside to myths. (2 Timothy 4:3-4).

When we stop teaching the truth of the Word of God, the church is no longer salt and light for God. Christianity will go into a decline. This is no more evident anywhere than in Europe. If we study the writings of church leaders throughout church history, we will find a number of men from different denominations who believed in predestination and election. A few of these are Saint Augustine, Martin Luther, John Calvin, Charles Spurgeon, and D. Martin Lloyd-Jones. Here we have five men from five different denominations who preached and taught predestination and election. In doing so, they were merely preaching and teaching what the Bible says.

> [27] And he will send his angels and gather his elect from the four winds, from the ends of the earth to the ends of the heavens. (Mark 13:27).

THE RELATIONSHIP
OF
THE HOLY SPIRIT
AND
THE CHRISTIAN

Hopefully you have examined yourself and have found that you are a Christian. Or possibly you found that you were not a Christian. If so, I hope you repented of your sins, put your trust in Christ to save you, and are now born again. If you did, you are a brand new Christian — a baby Christian, but don't keep it a secret. Tell others, particularly other Christians, so they can rejoice with you! Know also that there is rejoicing in heaven over your salvation.

> **¹⁰ In the same way, I tell you, there is rejoicing in the presence of the angels of God over one sinner who repents."** (Luke 15:10).

Let us now look at this wonderful relationship between God's Holy Spirit and the Christian. Let us look at who the Holy Spirit is, what He does, His work in the Christian, and His work through the Christian. The more we know and understand about this vital relationship, the more we will be prepared to live a victorious Christian life. However, let us be well aware that simply being prepared to live a victorious Christian life is not sufficient. One must apply that preparation and actually live it. If a person is always preparing to go on a wonderful vacation, but never does go, it would seem odd. It would also seem that the time and effort of preparing is a real waste. In the same way, the

Christian who prepares <u>to do</u> but never gets around <u>to doing,</u> is wasting all of that preparation. Let us then approach our discussion of the relationship between the Holy Spirit and the Christian with a view toward learning and preparing, but always with a commitment <u>to do</u> — to put into practice what we have learned and what we are prepared for. With this as our goal, let us begin by answering the question: Who is the Holy Spirit?

The Holy Spirit — The Third Person of The Trinity

As we seek to understand who the Holy Spirit is, we do not want to be confused by our lack of understanding of the Trinity.

The Bible teaches that there is one God who is three persons. No one can explain it, but God's Word teaches it; therefore, we believe it. For some Christians this can raise the question of whom to look to for direction and strength in their Christian walk. The answer is God. God the Father, God the Son, and God the Holy Spirit are one God. All three persons of the Godhead are divine and eternal and exist in the divine essence. They are not three gods but are the three persons of the one God. Though the word Trinity is not found in Scripture, it is used theologically to express the one essence eternally subsisting as three persons. These three are eternal, equal, and possess the same divine attributes. They are one in essence, in personality, and in will — three persons but one God. The one intelligence and the one will of the one God are expressed and exercised by the three persons. They each have their office and they are revealed in Scripture in a certain order of operation. The Father sends and works through the Son. The Father and Son send and work through the Spirit. Therefore, the one we speak of as indwelling believers is the Holy Spirit. The Holy Spirit is God in His fullness.

We speak of asking Christ to come into our hearts, which He does by sending His Holy Spirit to us. We also speak of being led by Christ or being led by God to do a certain thing. The Bible teaches that all three persons indwell us because the three are one.

Romans 8:9 and 1 Corinthians 6:19 are two of the verses that tell us that Christians are indwelt by the Holy Spirit.

> [9] You, however, are controlled not by the sinful nature but by the Spirit, if the Spirit of God lives in you. And if anyone does not have the Spirit of Christ, he does not belong to Christ. (Romans 8:9).

> [19] Do you not know that your body is a temple of the Holy Spirit, who is in you, whom you have received from God? You are not your own...
> (1 Corinthians 6:19).

Some examples that indicate we are indwelt by the Father and the Son are as follows:

> [4] There is one body and one Spirit— just as you were called to one hope when you were called— [5] one Lord, one faith, one baptism; [6] one God and Father of all, who is over all and through all and in all.
> (Ephesians 4:4-6).

> [20] I have been crucified with Christ and I no longer live, but Christ lives in me. (Galatians 2:20a).

> [4] Remain in me, and I will remain in you. No branch can bear fruit by itself; it must remain in the vine. Neither can you bear fruit unless you remain in me.
> (John 15:4).

> [23] Jesus replied, "If anyone loves me, he will obey my teaching. My Father will love him, and we will come to him and make our home with him.
> (John 14:23).

It is fair to conclude from Scripture that we are indwelt with the fullness of God: God the Father, God the Son, and God the Holy Spirit — not three gods but the three persons of the one God. Where one of the persons is, the other two are also there because there is only one God. And remember, our God is everywhere.

> [7] Where can I go from your Spirit? Where can I flee from your presence? [8] If I go up to the heavens, you are there; if I make my bed in the depths, you are there. (Psalm 139:7-8).

Let us not be confused about the Son, Jesus Christ. He walked on earth as fully God and fully man. As God, Christ has always existed — He is eternal God.

> [1] In the beginning was the Word, and the Word was with God, and the Word was God. [2] He was with God in the beginning. (John 1:1-2).

As man, Christ was born of a woman. However, He did not have a human father. His mother, Mary, was a virgin. Jesus Christ was conceived by the Holy Spirit.

> [18] This is how the birth of Jesus Christ came about: His mother Mary was pledged to be married to Joseph, but before they came together, she was found to be with child through the Holy Spirit. [19] Because Joseph her husband was a righteous man and did not want to expose her to public disgrace, he had in mind to divorce her quietly. [20] But after he had considered this, an angel of the Lord appeared to him in a dream and said, "Joseph son of David, do not be afraid to take Mary home as your wife, because what is conceived in her is from the Holy Spirit. [21] She will give birth to a son, and you are to give him the name Jesus, because he will save his people from their sins." [22] All this took place to fulfill what the Lord had said through the prophet: [23] "The virgin will be with child and will give birth to a son, and they will call him Immanuel"—which

> means, "God with us." [24] When Joseph woke up, he did what the angel of the Lord had commanded him and took Mary home as his wife. [25] But he had no union with her until she gave birth to a son. And he gave him the name Jesus. (Matthew 1:18-25).

Jesus was born as a baby like all men, and like all men He had to grow up before He became a man.

> [52] And Jesus grew in wisdom and stature, and in favor with God and men. (Luke 2:52).

When Christ walked on earth He was without sin. He fulfilled The Law perfectly.

> [14] Therefore, since we have a great high priest who has gone through the heavens, Jesus the Son of God, let us hold firmly to the faith we profess. [15] For we do not have a high priest who is unable to sympathize with our weaknesses, but we have one who has been tempted in every way, just as we are— yet was without sin. (Hebrews 4:14-15).

> [17] "Do not think that I have come to abolish the Law or the Prophets; I have not come to abolish them but to fulfill them. (Matthew 5:17).

Christ the man died — God cannot die. He is eternal. Christ was resurrected and now sits at the right hand of God the Father. Christ's body can only be in one place at a time. However, as fully God, the second person of the Trinity, He is everywhere. Even though all three persons of the one God are present all the time, we speak of God the Father as having the prominent role in Old Testament times. He spoke to Adam and Eve, Abraham, and others. When Christ walked on earth, He had the prominent role. From the day of Pentecost when the Holy Spirit came in power, He has had the prominent role. Therefore, it is to the Holy Spirit that we look to lead us, enable us, and empower us to do His will.

> [14...] because those who are led by the Spirit of God are sons of God. (Romans 8:14).

Characteristics of The Holy Spirit

We have seen that the Holy Spirit is not some impersonal force or power. He is God, the third person of the Trinity. The Holy Spirit has a personality in the same manner as the Father and the Son. Personal properties and actions are attributed to Him:

He has infinite intellect.

> [11] For who among men knows the thoughts of a man except the man's spirit within him? In the same way no one knows the thoughts of God except the Spirit of God. (1Corinthians 2:11).

He has a will.

> [11] All these are the work of one and the same Spirit, and he gives them to each one, just as he determines. (1 Corinthians 12:11).

> [4] God also testified to it by signs, wonders and various miracles, and gifts of the Holy Spirit distributed according to his will. (Hebrews 2:4).

He teaches.

> [11] "When you are brought before synagogues, rulers and authorities, do not worry about how you will defend yourselves or what you will say, [12] for the Holy Spirit will teach you at that time what you should say." (Luke 12:11-12).

> [13] This is what we speak, not in words taught us by human wisdom but in words taught by the Spirit, expressing spiritual truths in spiritual words. (1 Corinthians 2:13).

He speaks to people and through people.

> [1] The Spirit clearly says that in later times some will abandon the faith and follow deceiving spirits and things taught by demons. (1Timothy 4:1).

[15] In those days Peter stood up among the believers (a group numbering about a hundred and twenty) [16] and said, "Brothers, the Scripture had to be fulfilled which the Holy Spirit spoke long ago through the mouth of David concerning Judas, who served as guide for those who arrested Jesus... (Acts 1:15-16).

[19] While Peter was still thinking about the vision, the Spirit said to him, "Simon, three men are looking for you. [20] So get up and go downstairs. Do not hesitate to go with them, for I have sent them."
(Acts 10:19-20).

[23] I only know that in every city the Holy Spirit warns me that prison and hardships are facing me.
(Acts 20:23).

[17] "Be on your guard against men; they will hand you over to the local councils and flog you in their synagogues. [18] On my account you will be brought before governors and kings as witnesses to them and to the Gentiles. [19] But when they arrest you, do not worry about what to say or how to say it. At that time you will be given what to say, [20] for it will not be you speaking, but the Spirit of your Father speaking through you. (Matthew 10:17-20).

[29] The Spirit told Philip, "Go to that chariot and stay near it." (Acts 8:29).

He can be lied to.

[3] Then Peter said, "Ananias, how is it that Satan has so filled your heart that you have lied to the Holy Spirit and have kept for yourself some of the money you received for the land? (Acts 5:3).

He exerts authority.

[1] In the church at Antioch there were prophets and teachers: Barnabas, Simeon called Niger, Lucius of Cyrene, Manaen (who had been brought up with Herod the tetrarch) and Saul. [2] While they were worshiping the Lord and fasting, the Holy Spirit said, "Set apart for me Barnabas and Saul for the work to

which I have called them." [3] So after they had fasted and prayed, they placed their hands on them and sent them off. [4] The two of them, sent on their way by the Holy Spirit, went down to Seleucia and sailed from there to Cyprus. (Acts 13:1-4).

[22] "And now, compelled by the Spirit, I am going to Jerusalem, not knowing what will happen to me there. (Acts 20:22).

[28] Keep watch over yourselves and all the flock of which the Holy Spirit has made you overseers. (Acts 20:28a).

[12] The Spirit told me to have no hesitation about going with them. (Acts 11:12a).

He loves.

[30] I urge you, brothers, by our Lord Jesus Christ and by the love of the Spirit, to join me in my struggle by praying to God for me. (Romans 15:30).

He can be resisted.

[51] "You stiff-necked people, with uncircumcised hearts and ears! You are just like your fathers: You always resist the Holy Spirit! (Acts 7:51).

He can be grieved.

[10] Yet they rebelled and grieved his Holy Spirit. So he turned and became their enemy and he himself fought against them. (Isaiah 63:10).

[30] And do not grieve the Holy Spirit of God, with whom you were sealed for the day of redemption. (Ephesians 4:30).

Names and Symbols of The Holy Spirit

The Holy Spirit is referred to in Scripture as the Holy Ghost, Spirit of the Lord, Spirit of Christ, Spirit of God, Spirit of Truth, etc. Symbols such as wind, oil, fire, water, breath, and the finger of God are also used to indicate the Spirit. An example of water being used as a symbol of the Spirit is found in the Gospel of John.

> [37] On the last and greatest day of the Feast, Jesus stood and said in a loud voice, "If anyone is thirsty, let him come to me and drink. [38] Whoever believes in me, as the Scripture has said, streams of living water will flow from within him." [39] By this he meant the Spirit, whom those who believed in him were later to receive. Up to that time the Spirit had not been given, since Jesus had not yet been glorified. (John 7:37-39).

A dove is the symbol used when Jesus is baptized.

> [16] As soon as Jesus was baptized, he went up out of the water. At that moment heaven was opened, and he saw the Spirit of God descending like a dove and lighting on him. (Matthew 3:16).

Examples of The Holy Spirit in The Old Testament

The first reference to the Holy Spirit in the Bible is in the book of Genesis.

> [2] Now the earth was formless and empty, darkness was over the surface of the deep, and the Spirit of God was hovering over the waters. (Genesis 1:2).

The Holy Spirit's work and influence are seen throughout the Old Testament. For example:

> [1] Then the LORD said to Moses, [2] "See, I have chosen Bezalel son of Uri, the son of Hur, of the tribe of Judah, [3] and I have filled him with the Spirit of God, with skill, ability and knowledge in all kinds of crafts..." (Exodus 31:1-3).

> [17] I will come down and speak with you there, and I will take of the Spirit that is on you and put the Spirit

on them. They will help you carry the burden of the
people so that you will not have to carry it alone.
(Numbers 11:17).

[10] The Spirit of the LORD came upon him, so that he
became Israel's judge and went to war.
(Judges 3:10a).

[29] Then the Spirit of the LORD came upon Jephthah...
(Judges 11:29a).

[6] The Spirit of the LORD will come upon you in power,
and you will prophesy with them; and you will be
changed into a different person. [7] Once these signs
are fulfilled, do whatever your hand finds to do, for
God is with you. (1 Samuel 10:6-7).

[2] "The Spirit of the LORD spoke through me; his word
was on my tongue. (2 Samuel 23:2).

[20] You gave your good Spirit to instruct them. You
did not withhold your manna from their mouths, and
you gave them water for their thirst.
(Nehemiah 9:20).

[11] Do not cast me from your presence or take your
Holy Spirit from me. (Psalm 51:11).

Examples of The Holy Spirit in The New Testament

In the New Testament, we see much of the work and
the power of the Holy Spirit. John the Baptist was filled with
(controlled by) the Holy Spirit while still in his mother's
womb.

[15]...for he will be great in the sight of the Lord. He is
never to take wine or other fermented drink, and he
will be filled with the Holy Spirit even from birth.
(Luke 1:15).

Elizabeth (John's mother) and Zechariah (John's father)
were filled with the Holy Spirit.

[41] When Elizabeth heard Mary's greeting, the baby leaped in her womb, and Elizabeth was filled with the Holy Spirit. (Luke 1:41).

[67] His father Zechariah was filled with the Holy Spirit and prophesied: (Luke 1:67).

[1] When the day of Pentecost came, they were all together in one place. [2] Suddenly a sound like the blowing of a violent wind came from heaven and filled the whole house where they were sitting. [3] They saw what seemed to be tongues of fire that separated and came to rest on each of them. [4] All of them were filled with the Holy Spirit and began to speak in other tongues as the Spirit enabled them. (Acts 2:1-4).

[1] In those days when the number of disciples was increasing, the Grecian Jews among them complained against the Hebraic Jews because their widows were being overlooked in the daily distribution of food. [2] So the Twelve gathered all the disciples together and said, "It would not be right for us to neglect the ministry of the word of God in order to wait on tables. [3] Brothers, choose seven men from among you who are known to be full of the Spirit and wisdom. We will turn this responsibility over to them [4] and will give our attention to prayer and the ministry of the word." (Acts 6:1-4).

The Holy Spirit in The Life of Christ

The Holy Spirit was instrumental in the conception of Christ and in His life and ministry.

[35] The angel answered, "The Holy Spirit will come upon you, and the power of the Most High will overshadow you. So the holy one to be born will be called the Son of God. (Luke 1:35).

During the time Christ was on earth He was fully God and also fully man. However, He did His work on earth as man. He set aside being the Second Person of the Trinity that He might do His work as man. And, as man, He did His work in the power of the Holy Spirit. God gave Him the Spirit without limit.

> [5] Your attitude should be the same as that of Christ Jesus: [6] Who, being in very nature God, did not consider equality with God something to be grasped, [7] but made himself nothing, taking the very nature of a servant, being made in human likeness. [8] And being found in appearance as a man, he humbled himself and became obedient to death— even death on a cross! [9] Therefore God exalted him to the highest place and gave him the name that is above every name, [10] that at the name of Jesus every knee should bow, in heaven and on earth and under the earth, [11] and every tongue confess that Jesus Christ is Lord, to the glory of God the Father. (Philippians 2:5-11).

> [17] For this reason he had to be made like his brothers in every way, in order that he might become a merciful and faithful high priest in service to God, and that he might make atonement for the sins of the people. [18] Because he himself suffered when he was tempted, he is able to help those who are being tempted. (Hebrews 2:17-18).

> [34] For the one whom God has sent speaks the words of God, for God gives the Spirit without limit. (John 3:34).

Christ was anointed with the Holy Spirit.

> [38]…how God anointed Jesus of Nazareth with the Holy Spirit and power, and how he went around doing good and healing all who were under the power of the devil, because God was with him. (Acts 10:38).

Christ was full (under the control) of the Holy Spirit, and was led by the Holy Spirit when He faced Satan.

> [1] **Jesus, full of the Holy Spirit, returned from the Jordan and was led by the Spirit in the desert,** [2] **where for forty days he was tempted by the devil. He ate nothing during those days, and at the end of them he was hungry.** (Luke 4:1-2).

Christ, after facing Satan, returned to Galilee in the power of the Holy Spirit.

> [14] **Jesus returned to Galilee in the power of the Spirit, and news about him spread through the whole countryside.** (Luke 4:14).

Christ performed His ministry in the power of the Holy Spirit.

> [17] **The scroll of the prophet Isaiah was handed to him. Unrolling it, he found the place where it is written:** [18] **"The Spirit of the Lord is on me, because he has anointed me to preach good news to the poor. He has sent me to proclaim freedom for the prisoners and recovery of sight for the blind, to release the oppressed,** [19] **to proclaim the year of the Lord's favor."** [20] **Then he rolled up the scroll, gave it back to the attendant and sat down. The eyes of everyone in the synagogue were fastened on him,** [21] **and he began by saying to them, "Today this scripture is fulfilled in your hearing."** (Luke 4:17-21).

Christ offered Himself on the cross, through the power of the Holy Spirit.

> [14] **How much more, then, will the blood of Christ, who through the eternal Spirit offered himself unblemished to God, cleanse our consciences from acts that lead to death, so that we may serve the living God!** (Hebrews 9:14).

Christ was resurrected by the Holy Spirit.

> [4]**...and who through the Spirit of holiness was declared with power to be the Son of God by his resurrection from the dead: Jesus Christ our Lord.** (Romans 1:4).

> [11] And if the Spirit of him who raised Jesus from the dead is living in you, he who raised Christ from the dead will also give life to your mortal bodies through his Spirit, who lives in you. (Romans 8:11).

Christ gave instructions through the Holy Spirit.

> [2]...until the day he was taken up to heaven, after giving instructions through the Holy Spirit to the apostles he had chosen. (Acts 1:2).

The Indwelling Holy Spirit

One way the Holy Spirit glorifies Christ is by His work in and through Christians. He is the counselor or helper that Christ promised to send.

> [26] But the Counselor, the Holy Spirit, whom the Father will send in my name, will teach you all things and will remind you of everything I have said to you. (John 14:26).

> [5] "Now I am going to him who sent me, yet none of you asks me, 'Where are you going?' [6] Because I have said these things, you are filled with grief. [7] But I tell you the truth: It is for your good that I am going away. Unless I go away, the Counselor will not come to you; but if I go, I will send him to you. [8] When he comes, he will convict the world of guilt in regard to sin and righteousness and judgment: [9] in regard to sin, because men do not believe in me; [10] in regard to righteousness, because I am going to the Father, where you can see me no longer; [11] and in regard to judgment, because the prince of this world now stands condemned. [12] "I have much more to say to you, more than you can now bear. [13] But when he, the Spirit of truth, comes, he will guide you into all truth. He will not speak on his own; he will speak only what he hears, and he will tell you what is yet to come. (John 16:5-13).

> [16] And I will ask the Father, and he will give you another Counselor to be with you forever—[17] the

> Spirit of truth. The world cannot accept him,
> because it neither sees him nor knows him. But you
> know him, for he lives with you and will be in you.
> (John 14:16-17).

The above passages, and in particular John 14:16-17, have confused some Christians about how the Old Testament saints were saved. Did they not have the Holy Spirit? Yes, they did. What about Christ, did they believe in Him? Yes, they did, although they did not know His name. But they knew the Scriptures taught that there was a Messiah to come and He would save His people.

> [41] The first thing Andrew did was to find his brother Simon and tell him, "We have found the Messiah" (that is, the Christ). (John 1:41).

> [45] Philip found Nathanael and told him, "We have found the one Moses wrote about in the Law, and about whom the prophets also wrote—Jesus of Nazareth, the son of Joseph." (John 1:45).

> [25] Now there was a man in Jerusalem called Simeon, who was righteous and devout. He was waiting for the consolation of Israel, and the Holy Spirit was upon him. [26] It had been revealed to him by the Holy Spirit that he would not die before he had seen the Lord's Christ. [27] Moved by the Spirit, he went into the temple courts. When the parents brought in the child Jesus to do for him what the custom of the Law required, [28] Simeon took him in his arms and praised God, saying: [29] "Sovereign Lord, as you have promised, you now dismiss your servant in peace. [30] For my eyes have seen your salvation, [31] which you have prepared in the sight of all people, [32] a light for revelation to the Gentiles and for glory to your people Israel." (Luke 2:25-32).

Christ said Abraham understood He was coming.

> [56] Your father Abraham rejoiced at the thought of seeing my day; he saw it and was glad." (John 8:56).

During the time that Christ walked on earth, the Scriptures that the Jews had was our Old Testament. Christ says they testified about Him.

> [39] **You diligently study the Scriptures because you think that by them you possess eternal life. These are the Scriptures that testify about me, [40] yet you refuse to come to me to have life.** (John 5:39-40).

The teaching of the Bible is clear; the Old Testament saints were saved just as we are. They looked forward to a Savior that <u>was yet to come</u> and we look back at a Savior that <u>has already come</u>. In both cases, it is a matter of being saved by grace. It is a free gift, unearned, and undeserved. God freely gives us salvation out of His love and mercy.

If you wonder how the Old Testament saints understood God's plan from their Scriptures when so many people today don't understand the New Testament (which seems much clearer), let me hasten to say it was by the Holy Spirit. The Old Testament believers and the New Testament believers all believe because they have been regenerated and are indwelt by the Holy Spirit. As I said, some Christians are confused over John 14:16-7. John 7:39 also adds to their confusion. This will be explained over the next several pages.

> [39] **By this he meant the Spirit, whom those who believed in him were later to receive. Up to that time the Spirit had not been given, since Jesus had not yet been glorified.** (John 7:39).

On the surface it might seem that people did not have the Holy Spirit until after Pentecost, but that is not what is being taught. It is clear from what the Bible teaches and from what Christ Himself said, that all who are saved are saved by being regenerated (made spiritually alive) by the Holy Spirit. This includes all of mankind, those who have been saved in the past and those who will be saved in the future. People who lived before Christ came, while He was on earth, and after His ascension to heaven are all the same. We all have a sinful nature. None of us can believe and trust Christ because, humanly speaking, we are unable to understand and therefore have no desire to trust Him. People living before Pentecost were no exception.

> [14] The man without the Spirit does not accept the things that come from the Spirit of God, for they are foolishness to him, and he cannot understand them, because they are spiritually discerned.
> (1 Corinthians 2:14).

Now, if man without the Spirit is unable to believe because he doesn't have the Spirit and is therefore operating in his human nature, which is sinful, then he is not able to please God. God wants men to repent and be saved, but a man without the Spirit will not because he cannot.

> [7] the sinful mind is hostile to God. It does not submit to God's law, nor can it do so. [8] Those controlled by the sinful nature cannot please God. (Romans 8:7-8).

It is only by God giving us the Holy Spirit that we are enabled to understand and are moved to believe and trust Christ.

> [12] We have not received the spirit of the world but the Spirit who is from God, that we may understand what God has freely given us.
> (1 Corinthians 2:12).

Christ makes it clear that man must be made spiritually alive — he must be born spiritually. Christ refers to this spiritual birth as being born again. It is when the Holy Spirit regenerates a man and comes to live within the man. In addition to our physical birth, we must experience a spiritual birth if we hope to go to heaven; therefore, the term "be born again." This term is often referred to as being born from above. In reality that is what takes place.

> [1] Now there was a man of the Pharisees named Nicodemus, a member of the Jewish ruling council.
> [2] He came to Jesus at night and said, "Rabbi, we

> know you are a teacher who has come from God. For
> no one could perform the miraculous signs you are
> doing if God were not with him." [3] In reply Jesus
> declared, "I tell you the truth, no one can see the
> kingdom of God unless he is born again." [4] "How
> can a man be born when he is old?" Nicodemus
> asked. "Surely he cannot enter a second time into
> his mother's womb to be born!" [5] Jesus answered, "I
> tell you the truth, no one can enter the kingdom of
> God unless he is born of water and the Spirit. [6] Flesh
> gives birth to flesh, but the Spirit gives birth to spirit.
> [7] You should not be surprised at my saying, 'You
> must be born again.' [8] The wind blows wherever it
> pleases. You hear its sound, but you cannot tell
> where it comes from or where it is going. So it is
> with everyone born of the Spirit." [9] "How can this
> be?" Nicodemus asked. [10] "You are Israel's teacher,"
> said Jesus, "and do you not understand these
> things? (John 3:1-10).

Let us note that Jesus is speaking here before the day
of Pentecost. He states emphatically that no one can enter
the kingdom of God unless he has been born again.
He even rebukes the Pharisee Nicodemus for not knowing
this because Nicodemus was a leading teacher of the Old
Testament Jews.

Let us note again that Jesus told the 72 disciples whom
He had sent out to rejoice that their names were written in
heaven. That means they were saved — had been born of
the Spirit before Pentecost.

> [20] However, do not rejoice that the spirits submit to
> you, but rejoice that your names are written in
> heaven." (Luke 10:20).

When Jesus washed His disciples' feet He told Peter he
was clean. He was not speaking of physical cleanliness but
of spiritual cleanliness. He meant that Peter was saved. This
too was before Pentecost.

> [1] It was just before the Passover Feast. Jesus knew
> that the time had come for him to leave this world

and go to the Father. Having loved his own who were in the world, he now showed them the full extent of his love. [2] The evening meal was being served, and the devil had already prompted Judas Iscariot, son of Simon, to betray Jesus. [3] Jesus knew that the Father had put all things under his power, and that he had come from God and was returning to God; [4] so he got up from the meal, took off his outer clothing, and wrapped a towel around his waist. [5] After that, he poured water into a basin and began to wash his disciples' feet, drying them with the towel that was wrapped around him. [6] He came to Simon Peter, who said to him, "Lord, are you going to wash my feet?" [7] Jesus replied, "You do not realize now what I am doing, but later you will understand." [8] "No," said Peter, "you shall never wash my feet." Jesus answered, "Unless I wash you, you have no part with me." [9] "Then, Lord," Simon Peter replied, "not just my feet but my hands and my head as well!" [10] Jesus answered, "A person who has had a bath needs only to wash his feet; his whole body is clean. And you are clean, though not every one of you." [11] For he knew who was going to betray him, and that was why he said not every one was clean. (John 13:1-11).

Peter tells us that the prophets who spoke about salvation were indwelt by the Holy Spirit.

[10] Concerning this salvation, the prophets, who spoke of the grace that was to come to you, searched intently and with the greatest care, [11] trying to find out the time and circumstances to which the Spirit of Christ in them was pointing when he predicted the sufferings of Christ and the glories that would follow. (1 Peter 1:10-11).

We know there is only one true gospel and only one Savior, Jesus Christ. All who are saved in any age belong to Christ. Paul says that if you belong to Christ you will have the Holy Spirit.

[9] You, however, are controlled not by the sinful nature but by the Spirit, if the Spirit of God lives in

> **you. And if anyone does not have the Spirit of Christ, he does not belong to Christ.** (Romans 8:9).

We have seen in Scripture that the Holy Spirit indwells all believers. This should help to clear up the confusion of John 14:16-17 and John 7:39 concerning the Spirit.

Let us now see what is meant by the expression "the Spirit had not been given" in John 7:39. What the Bible teaches is that at Pentecost the Holy Spirit was poured out as the prophet Joel had prophesied. The Spirit had always been at work in and through God's people but now His work was more widespread and more clearly seen. It was as though from heaven God had poured out the Spirit on mankind.

> [28] **'And afterward, I will pour out my Spirit on all people. Your sons and daughters will prophesy, your old men will dream dreams, your young men will see visions.** [29] **Even on my servants, both men and women, I will pour out my Spirit in those days.** (Joel 2:28-29).

At Pentecost the Holy Spirit came in power. There was a very visible display of the fact that He was at work. Gentiles as well as Jews were being saved, and Christianity was spreading across the known world.

To shed further light on the fact that the Holy Spirit was working to regenerate the Old Testament saints just as He does us today, let us see what three well-respected theologians have to say about it.

J. C. Ryle in his Expository Thoughts on John had this to say about John 7:39:

> *Before our Lord died and rose again and ascended, the Holy Ghost was, and had been from all eternity, one with the Father and the Son, a distinct Person, of equal power and authority, very and eternal God.*

But He had not revealed Himself so fully to those whose hearts He dwelt in as He did after the ascension; and He had not come down in person on the Gentile world, or sent forth the Gospel to all mankind with rivers of blessing, as He did when Paul and Barnabas were "sent forth by the Holy Ghost." (Acts 13:4) In a word, the dispensation of the Spirit had not yet begun.

When therefore we read "the Holy Ghost was not," we need not be stumbled by the expression. It simply means "He was not fully manifested and poured out on the Church." Peter, and James, and John, no doubt, had the Spirit now, when our Lord was speaking. But they had Him much more fully after our Lord was glorified. This explains the meaning of the passage before us.

Referring to this, John Calvin said the following:

For the Spirit was not yet. The Spirit is eternal, as we know. But the Evangelist is saying that, so long as Christ dwelt in the world in the lowly form of a Servant, that grace of the Spirit which was poured out on men after the resurrection of Christ had not come forth openly. And indeed he is speaking comparatively, as when the New Testament is compared to the Old. God promises His Spirit to believers as if He had never given Him to the Fathers. At that time the disciples had undoubtedly already received the firstfruits of the Spirit. For where does faith come from if not from the Spirit? The Evangelist then does not simply deny that the grace of the Spirit was revealed to believers before the death of Christ, but that it was not yet so bright and clear, as it would be afterwards. For the chief glory of Christ's Kingdom is that He governs the Church by His Spirit. But He entered into the lawful and, as it were, ceremonial possession of His Kingdom when He was exalted to the right hand of the Father. So there is nothing surprising in His delaying the full manifestation of the Spirit until then.

B. B. Warfield had this to say about John 7:39:

There yet remains an important query which we cannot pass wholly by. We have seen the rich development of the doctrine of the Spirit in the Old Testament. We have seen the testimony the Old Testament bears to the activity of the Spirit of God throughout the old dispensation. What then is meant by calling the new dispensation the dispensation of the Spirit? What does John (7:39) mean by saying that the Spirit was not yet given because Jesus was not yet glorified? What our Lord Himself, when He promised the comforter, by saying that the Comforter would not come until He went away and sent Him (John 16:7); and by breathing on His disciples, saying, "Receive ye the Holy Spirit" (John 20:22)? What did the descent of the Spirit at Pentecost mean, when He came to inaugurate the dispensation of the Spirit? It cannot be meant that the Spirit was not active in the old dispensation. We have already seen that the New Testament writers themselves represent Him to have been active in the old dispensation in all the varieties of activity with which He is active in the new.

The Spirit worked in Providence no less universally then than now. He abode in the Church not less really then than now. He wrought in the hearts of God's people not less prevalently then than now. All the good that was in the world was then as now due to Him. All the hope of God's Church then as now depended on Him. Every grace of the godly life then as now was a fruit of His working.

Being indwelt by the Holy Spirit is one thing, but being controlled by the Holy Spirit is another. All Christians are indwelt by the Holy Spirit, yet all Christians sin. When a Christian sins, he is in control of his desires and actions. The Holy Spirit will not lead him to sin. While under His control, he can be tempted to sin, but will not succumb to the temptation. The Holy Spirit will never empower him to sin, but will always empower him to resist sin and to do good works. Just as the unbeliever must trust Christ to be saved, the believer must trust the Holy Spirit to control his thoughts, desires, and actions to live a fruitful Christian life. Without trust, the unbeliever will not be saved. Without trust, the believer will not be controlled. "We have not because we ask not." If we don't ask the Holy Spirit to control us, our sinful nature will control us.

Just as the unbeliever must come to the realization that without Christ, he is a lost sinner and that Christ alone can save him, so must the Christian come to the realization that in his own strength, he is utterly unable to live the Christian life in a manner pleasing to God. The Holy Spirit alone can provide the power and enable the Christian to please God.

The Worldly Acting Christian

There are many Christians who understand very little about the work of the Holy Spirit in their lives. There are others who do not put into practice the knowledge and understanding that they have — often ignoring or resisting the prompting of the Spirit. As a result, there are many Christians who fall into the category that is known as worldly. The worldly Christian is one who acts much like those of the world.

[1] Brothers, I could not address you as spiritual but as worldly—mere infants in Christ. [2] I gave you milk, not solid food, for you were not yet ready for it. Indeed, you are still not ready. [3] You are still worldly.

For since there is jealousy and quarreling among you, are you not worldly? Are you not acting like mere men? (1 Corinthians 3:1-3).

The worldly Christian is one who is more influenced by the flesh than the Spirit; therefore, he thinks and acts so much like the unbeliever that one can see little, if any, difference between them. If Satan cannot keep a man from coming to Christ, he will try to keep him from living for Christ. He will try to keep him walking in the flesh — keep him worldly.

The unsaved man does not have the Holy Spirit. He is always motivated by his human nature. The Bible makes it clear that our human nature is sinful. Actions that stem from it cannot please God.

[8] **Those controlled by the sinful nature cannot please God.** (Romans 8:8).

Being controlled by his sinful nature is why so much of the time the worldly Christian does not please God. Although he is indwelt by the Spirit, he lives most of the time controlled by his human nature rather than by the Spirit. Because the trend of the worldly Christian's life is one of doing his own thing, he lives a life of guilt and defeat. Although he has a relationship with God, he seldom enjoys fellowship with Him. He misses out on the peace and joy that only come with submission to God's Holy Spirit. Anyone who is content to be a worldly Christian is on dangerous ground. He is skating on thin ice. If in his heart he is willing to be a worldly Christian, he may not have a changed heart — he may not even be a Christian. He may be self-deceived — thinking he is going to heaven but actually is on his way to hell.

On the other hand, the spiritual man is seeking to live as the Holy Spirit leads him. He does not do this perfectly though, as his sinful nature is prone to exert itself from time to time. However, the trend of his life is one of living under the control of the Holy Spirit.

We often see new Christians who, having just received Christ, are so elated that they blindly charge out to do something for God. Often they think they are winning favor in God's eyes. Humanly speaking, these intentions are good. However, even when in ignorance we charge out in our own strength to do what we think is a good thing, it does not please God because the Holy Spirit is not leading us.

Works done in the flesh do not please God before we are saved, and they do not please God after we are saved. Only works done in faith please God. Only those works done under the guidance and enabling of the Holy Spirit will please Him.

Paul understood it to be this way and tells us in Galatians that as we are made spiritually alive by the Spirit, we are to walk (live) under the control of the Spirit.

> [25] **Since we live by the Spirit, let us keep in step with the Spirit** (Galatians 5:25).

Because so much depends on our understanding and practice of letting the Holy Spirit control our lives, let us look further at His work in our lives.

The Holy Spirit in Salvation

The teaching of Scripture is that we were once spiritually dead and that God gave us spiritual life.

> [5]**…he saved us, not because of righteous things we had done, but because of his mercy. He saved us through the washing of rebirth and renewal by the Holy Spirit…** (Titus 3:5).

> [4] **But because of his great love for us, God, who is rich in mercy,** [5] **made us alive with Christ even when we were dead in transgressions—it is by grace you have been saved.** (Ephesians 2:4-5).

At the time of spiritual birth, the Holy Spirit regenerates man and brings about the new birth. Just as there was a time when we did not have physical life but were born into the world without any effort on our part, there was also a time when we did not have spiritual life but were born into the Kingdom of God without effort on our part. We were given spiritual life; we were born again; we were saved.

The regeneration of man is the work of the Holy Spirit. The Holy Spirit applies the Word of God to our lives and brings about our spiritual birth. The Apostle John points out that our spiritual birth is the work of God.

> [12] **Yet to all who received him, to those who believed in his name, he gave the right to become children of God—** [13] **children born not of natural descent, nor of human decision or a husband's will, but born of God...** (John 1:12-13).

We see that those who are children of God are not children because of who their ancestors were, or because their parents are Christians. They are not God's children by human decision (a human plan, human sex drive, a husband's will to have an heir to his name), but because they have been born of God the Holy Spirit. All people are creatures of God, but only those who have been born again are children of God.

Several things happen at the time of our spiritual birth:

1. The moment we are born again (saved), the Holy Spirit comes to actually dwell within the body and life of the Christian.

> [9] **You, however, are controlled not by the sinful nature but by the Spirit, if the Spirit of God lives in you. And if anyone does not have the Spirit of Christ, he does not belong to Christ.** (Romans 8:9).
>
> [19] **Do you not know that your body is a temple of the Holy Spirit, who is in you, whom you have received from God? You are not your own...** (1 Corinthians 6:19).
>
> [13] **We know that we live in him and he in us, because he has given us of his Spirit.** (1 John 4:13).

2. We receive the Holy Spirit as a gift from God.

> [38] Peter replied, "Repent and be baptized, every one of you, in the name of Jesus Christ for the forgiveness of your sins. And you will receive the gift of the Holy Spirit. (Acts 2:38).

> [44] While Peter was still speaking these words, the Holy Spirit came on all who heard the message. [45] The circumcised believers who had come with Peter were astonished that the gift of the Holy Spirit had been poured out even on the Gentiles.
> (Acts 10:44-45).

This wonderful gift from God is passed by when a man rejects Christ. When a man refuses God's offer of salvation, he is not only turning down the opportunity of going to heaven, but he is also turning down the gift of the Holy Spirit. Christians should reflect on how wonderful this gift is. The Holy Spirit not only gives us direction and power to live the Christian life, but He also fellowships with us as He works in our life. This is sweet fellowship with God. He speaks to us through His Word and His promptings, and we speak to Him through our thoughts and verbal expressions. Do we fellowship with the Holy Spirit? Do we ask Him questions? Do we thank Him and praise Him for working in us? Do we ask Him to use us — to work through us? As Christians we should do this all through the day. If we have the gift of the Spirit, we should seek fellowship with Him. If we are not doing this, something is wrong with us.

> [14] May the grace of the Lord Jesus Christ, and the love of God, and the fellowship of the Holy Spirit be with you all. (2 Corinthians 13:14).

3. The Holy Spirit seals every Christian into Christ.

> [13] And you also were included in Christ when you heard the word of truth, the gospel of your salvation. Having believed, you were marked in him with a seal, the promised Holy Spirit... (Ephesians 1:13).

4. The Holy Spirit is the deposit or guarantee of the inheritance that each Christian will one day receive.

   [5] Now it is God who has made us for this very purpose and has given us the Spirit as a deposit, guaranteeing what is to come. (2 Corinthians 5:5).

   [14]...who is a deposit guaranteeing our inheritance until the redemption of those who are God's possession—to the praise of his glory. (Ephesians 1:14).

5. We are baptized into the body of Christ by Christ, who uses the Holy Spirit as His agent.

   [8] I baptize you with water, but he will baptize you with the Holy Spirit." (Mark 1:8).

   [13] For we were all baptized by one Spirit into one body—whether Jews or Greeks, slave or free—and we were all given the one Spirit to drink. (1 Corinthians 12:13).

The baptism of the Holy Spirit is something that is done at the time we are saved. It has nothing to do with water baptism — which does not save us. It has nothing to do with whether or not we speak in tongues. At the moment we are saved we are regenerated, indwelt, sealed, guaranteed, and baptized by the Holy Spirit. In addition to all of this, we enjoy the wonderful blessing of being set free. We had been held captive to a works oriented salvation, and we were in bondage to sin. We could do nothing but sin. Now we are free from the power of sin. We did not know God, and now we can commune with God. When we were given the Spirit we were given freedom.

   [17] Now the Lord is the Spirit, and where the Spirit of the Lord is, there is freedom. (2 Corinthians 3:17).

In bringing us to accept Christ, The Holy Spirit works in us in such a manner that no violence is done to our wills. He does not force us to do anything against our wills; rather He brings about a change of our wills. Without the Spirit's work, we would never come to Christ.

There are many well-taught people whom the Spirit has never drawn to Christ. They know the books, history, and characters of the Bible, but they do not know its truth. They do not know Christ personally and will not know Him, unless God the Holy Spirit reveals Him to them.

> [43] "Stop grumbling among yourselves," Jesus answered. [44] "No one can come to me unless the Father who sent me draws him, and I will raise him up at the last day. [45] It is written in the Prophets: 'They will all be taught by God.' Everyone who listens to the Father and learns from him comes to me. (John 6:43-45).

Regardless of how clearly the Gospel is presented to people or how many times they hear it, they will not believe it unless the Holy Spirit applies it to their hearts. In fact, even if someone returns from the dead to witness to them, they still will not believe if the Holy Spirit has not enabled them to believe God's Word. Christ tells us this is the case in the story of the rich man and Lazarus.

> [19] "There was a rich man who was dressed in purple and fine linen and lived in luxury every day. [20] At his gate was laid a beggar named Lazarus, covered with sores [21] and longing to eat what fell from the rich man's table. Even the dogs came and licked his sores. [22] "The time came when the beggar died and the angels carried him to Abraham's side. The rich man also died and was buried. [23] In hell, where he was in torment, he looked up and saw Abraham far away, with Lazarus by his side. [24] So he called to him, 'Father Abraham, have pity on me and send Lazarus to dip the tip of his finger in water and cool my tongue, because I am in agony in this fire.' [25] "But Abraham replied, 'Son, remember that in your lifetime you received your good things, while Lazarus received bad things, but now he is comforted here and you are in agony. [26]

And besides all this, between us and you a great chasm has been fixed, so that those who want to go from here to you cannot, nor can anyone cross over from there to us.' [27] "He answered, 'Then I beg you, father, send Lazarus to my father's house, [28] for I have five brothers. Let him warn them, so that they will not also come to this place of torment.' [29] "Abraham replied, 'They have Moses and the Prophets; let them listen to them.' [30] "'No, father Abraham,' he said, 'but if someone from the dead goes to them, they will repent.' [31] "He said to him, 'If they do not listen to Moses and the Prophets, they will not be convinced even if someone rises from the dead.'" (Luke 16:19-31).

This story brings home how truly helpless we are to come to Christ and how totally dependent we are on the Holy Spirit to give us spiritual life. Just as the physically dead do not respond to physical stimuli, so the spiritually dead do not respond to spiritual stimuli. The physically dead can be cut, poked, and exposed to loud noise, heat, and cold with no response. The spiritually dead can hear good preaching, read the Bible, be witnessed to, and listen to Christian tapes with no spiritual response. They are dead, and the dead do not respond. Being dead, they can do nothing to gain life — it must be given to them by the regenerating work of the Holy Spirit.

The more understanding we have of this truth the more we will appreciate the miracle of the new birth. Raising the spiritually dead to spiritual life requires the supernatural work of God, just as raising the physically dead to physical life does. Both of these show the power of God. It is this same power that indwells us and works in and through us. It is the same power that raised Christ from the dead.

[19]...and his incomparably great power for us who believe. That power is like the working of his mighty strength, [20] which he exerted in Christ when he raised him from the dead and seated him at his right hand in the heavenly realms.... (Ephesians 1:19-20).

Enabling Power of The Holy Spirit

Just as our salvation is a miracle, so is the sustaining of our Christian life. One becomes a Christian through the supernatural work of God, and one remains a Christian through His supernatural work.

> [3] **His divine power has given us everything we need for life and godliness through our knowledge of him who called us by his own glory and goodness.** (2 Peter 1:3).

> [16] **I pray that out of his glorious riches he may strengthen you with power through his Spirit in your inner being...** (Ephesians 3:16).

There is not a person who belongs to Christ who came to that relationship through their own power. It was through the work of the Holy Spirit. In the same way, no one can live as God commands except by the power of the Holy Spirit. Apart from the Spirit, the Christian can do nothing.

> [5] **"I am the vine; you are the branches. If a man remains in me and I in him, he will bear much fruit; apart from me you can do nothing.** (John 15:5).

The above verse does not mean that apart from Christ the unsaved man cannot achieve great success in this world. But it does mean that the unsaved man cannot do anything that pleases Christ. Furthermore, it also means that what the Christian does under the control of his human nature does not please God. The man who does not know Christ has no faith. The Christian has faith, but when he acts apart from Christ he is acting in the flesh instead of in the power of the Spirit; he is not acting in faith. In both cases their actions are not pleasing to God because in both cases they are done without faith.

> [6] **And without faith it is impossible to please God...** (Hebrews 11:6).

The Spirit is the enabling power of the Christian.

> [8] But you will receive power when the Holy Spirit comes on you; and you will be my witnesses in Jerusalem, and in all Judea and Samaria, and to the ends of the earth." (Acts 1:8).

> [20] Now to him who is able to do immeasurably more than all we ask or imagine, according to his power that is at work within us... (Ephesians 3:20).

Earlier in this book we looked at a number of verses that showed that Christ did His work under the control, and in the power of the Holy Spirit. In an effort to press the importance of our submitting to the control of the Holy Spirit let us look at two more examples of God working through Christ.

> [10] Don't you believe that I am in the Father, and that the Father is in me? The words I say to you are not just my own. Rather, it is the Father, living in me, who is doing his work. [11] Believe me when I say that I am in the Father and the Father is in me; or at least believe on the evidence of the miracles themselves. (John 14:10-11).

> [22] "Men of Israel, listen to this: Jesus of Nazareth was a man accredited by God to you by miracles, wonders and signs, which God did among you through him, as you yourselves know. (Acts 2:22).

If it was necessary for Christ to do His work in the power of the Holy Spirit, can we possibly expect to do our work without the power of the Holy Spirit?

We have numerous commands from God on what to do and what not to do. In fact, we have so many that new Christians often do not know how to start living their new lives. However, if we obey the command to be controlled by the Spirit, He will lead us and empower us to obey the other commands. Our obedience to this one command is the key to our obedience to all the others. With this being true, it is easy to see that the biggest obstacle to our living as God would have us live, and doing the work that God would have us do, is ourselves. It is our failure to yield the control of our lives to the Holy Spirit. God is perfectly capable of handling all external circumstances. He can open and close doors. He can cause people and events to work in cooperation with us and to assist us. It is our own selfish hearts, our refusal to deny self and follow Him in a consistent manner that hinders His work. Due to our sinful nature, living life under the control of the Holy Spirit is difficult, even when we are making a real effort to do so. It will not happen if we are not willing to work at it. It must be given top priority. If it is, all else will follow as God intends.

The Holy Spirit and Righteous Living

We should not only seek to enter the kingdom but also seek the righteousness expected of those who do enter it. Heaven should be our destination, and holiness should be the road we travel.

> [14]...**without holiness no one will see the Lord.** (Hebrews 12:1).

Too often, we Christians have a false sense of what it means to be righteous. As a result, we substitute the energy of the flesh, the wisdom of the flesh, and the excitement of the flesh for the righteousness of God. Works done in the flesh are works that are done without the Spirit's command, direction, or permission. From the human perspective, they may be successful, but they do not please God. They are sin.

The only way we can live a righteous life is by the Holy Spirit. The command to be controlled by the Holy Spirit is not an abstract spiritual phrase — it is a concrete spiritual reality. Just as salvation is available to and commanded of the unsaved, being controlled by the Holy Spirit is available to and commanded of the Christian. In both cases, those who reject the offer and refuse to obey the command are held accountable by God.

The Spirit of Christ Within Us

We know that Christ, by the Holy Spirit, lives in His people to continue His work on earth. Therefore, we need to realize that each of us shares his body with Christ.

> [20] **I have been crucified with Christ and I no longer live, but Christ lives in me. The life I live in the body, I live by faith in the Son of God, who loved me and gave himself for me.** (Galatians 2:20).

When we are under the control of our human nature, we are using our body and denying Christ the use of it. When we are under the control of the Holy Spirit, Christ is using our body, and we enjoy the benefits and blessings that come with His use. It is truly a blessing to be controlled by the Holy Spirit. More importantly, it is our duty to be. The Holy Spirit is not here to empower us to do what we choose to do for God. He is here to empower us to do what God wants done. We do not use the Holy Spirit, but He uses us. God does not need us to do anything for Him, but we need Him to do everything for us. As the Israelites were dependent on God for the manna from heaven to maintain their physical life, we are dependent on the Holy Spirit to maintain our spiritual life. When we seek to do that which we feel led to do in His power, we are only limited in what we can do by what God has decreed for us to do. We find that the Christian life becomes a real adventure.

The Holy Spirit is our only hope for living the Christian life; therefore, we certainly want to be careful not to do anything that will prevent His working in us.

> [19] **Do not put out the Spirit's fire...**
> (1 Thessalonians 5:19).

We can quench the Spirit's fire by sinful thoughts and actions. However, what can also be crippling to our Christian walk — and is so commonplace among Christians today —

is letting the fire diminish for lack of fuel. If we ignore the Spirit's presence, do not act at His prompting, neglect church, prayer, Bible study, and other graces that strengthen our faith, the fire will abate and our spiritual life will atrophy. We can be spiritual Christians at times. At other times we can quench the Spirit's work in our lives — even to the degree that we think, talk, and act so different that we seem to be two different people. In essence, we are led by two different persons at different times. We are either led by our sinful nature (the flesh) or by God the Holy Spirit. The one leading us determines our actions. We either suffer the consequences or enjoy the rewards, depending on who is doing the leading.

> [5] **Those who live according to the sinful nature have their minds set on what that nature desires; but those who live in accordance with the Spirit have their minds set on what the Spirit desires. [6] The mind of sinful man is death, but the mind controlled by the Spirit is life and peace...** (Romans 8:5-6).

> [7] **Do not be deceived: God cannot be mocked. A man reaps what he sows. [8] The one who sows to please his sinful nature, from that nature will reap destruction; the one who sows to please the Spirit, from the Spirit will reap eternal life.** (Galatians 6:7-8).

When we live according to the flesh we not only rationalize and make allowances for our sins, but we actually make provision for them. To live according to the Spirit we must yield to the Spirit, and He will lead us from there.

The Holy Spirit and Bible Study

The Holy Spirit and the Word of God go hand in hand. They both have a part in our salvation, and they both have a part in our sanctification. As the Spirit uses the Word in our lives, we grow in the grace and knowledge of our Lord Jesus Christ. Therefore, we can be sure of one thing, the Spirit will lead us to study the Word. If we are not studying the Word, it should raise a red flag in our heart and mind. When we study we should ask the Spirit to give us understanding. Studying the Word without the illumination of the Holy Spirit profits us very little. However, studying under the guidance and light of the Spirit is life changing. The written Word becomes a living Word under the illumination of the Holy Spirit. The Holy Spirit uses the Word of God to mold our character much as a craftsman uses an instrument. In fact, the Word is called the sword of the Spirit. If we are not studying the Word of God we are not being led by the Spirit of God.

> [17] **Take the helmet of salvation and the sword of the Spirit, which is the word of God.** (Ephesians 6:17).

> [12] **For the word of God is living and active. Sharper than any double-edged sword, it penetrates even to dividing soul and spirit, joints and marrow; it judges the thoughts and attitudes of the heart.**
> (Hebrews 4:12).

God's Word is the truth, and the Holy Spirit teaches us the truth.

> [17] **Sanctify them by the truth; your word is truth.**
> (John 17:17).

> [13] **But when he, the Spirit of truth, comes, he will guide you into all truth.** (John 16:13a).

This last verse tells us that it is the Holy Spirit who will guide us into all truth. So when you are in a Bible study or in church listening to a sermon, who is teaching you the truth? Is it the teacher of the Bible study or the pastor preaching the sermon? No, it is the Holy Spirit taking what is being said and convincing you that it is true or that it is not true. It is a blessing from God to have gifted teachers and preachers who know the Bible. However, we still should compare what they say with Scriptures to see if it is true. That is what the Bereans did when they heard the Apostle Paul preach.

> [11] Now the Bereans were of more noble character than the Thessalonians, for they received the message with great eagerness and examined the Scriptures every day to see if what Paul said was true. (Acts 17:11).

If we study God's Word and ask the Holy Spirit to give us understanding as we study, we hopefully will avoid two errors that some individuals and some churches fall into. These two errors are legalism and antinomianism. They are not only in opposition to what the Bible teaches, but they are also in direct opposition to each other. You might say they are two opposite extremes and the truth is somewhere between them. Let us consider legalism first.

Those who adhere to legalism not only distort and exaggerate the commands of God's moral law, but they also add their own commands. They often make up their rules of what they can or cannot do based on what they see happening in the culture, rather than what the Bible says.

> [13] The Lord says: "These people come near to me with their mouth and honor me with their lips, but their hearts are far from me. Their worship of me is made up only of rules taught by men. (Isaiah 29:13).

> [20] Since you died with Christ to the basic principles of this world, why, as though you still belonged to it, do you submit to its rules: [21] "Do not handle! Do not taste! Do not touch!"? [22] These are all destined to perish with use, because they are based on human commands and teachings. (Colossians 2:20-22).

Legalism leads to pride. Man-made rules are kept in the strength of the flesh and one sees himself doing what others either cannot or will not do. The legalist may profess to be saved by grace, but he gives the appearance of working to stay saved — even if he is not working to be saved.

Regardless, legalism carried far enough certainly raises a question about salvation.

On the other hand, antinomianism is a belief that faith in Christ is all that is necessary, and that if we have faith we can live as we wish. In other words, if we are saved we can do whatever we want to do. God's moral law is not binding on us. The antinomian thinks that if he prays a prayer to receive Christ that nothing else is required of him. He seems to be unaware that he is to do good works, bear fruit, and be holy.

> [10] **For we are God's workmanship, created in Christ Jesus to do good works, which God prepared in advance for us to do.** (Ephesians 2:10).

> [1] **"I am the true vine, and my Father is the gardener.** [2] **He cuts off every branch in me that bears no fruit, while every branch that does bear fruit he prunes so that it will be even more fruitful.** (John 15:1-2).

> [15] **But just as he who called you is holy, so be holy in all you do;** [16] **for it is written: "Be holy, because I am holy."** (1 Peter 1:15-16).

The antinomian may think he has faith, but his faith is dead — it will not save him.

> [14] **What good is it, my brothers, if a man claims to have faith but has no deeds? Can such faith save him?** [15] **Suppose a brother or sister is without clothes and daily food.** [16] **If one of you says to him, "Go, I wish you well; keep warm and well fed," but does nothing about his physical needs, what good is it?** [17] **In the same way, faith by itself, if it is not accompanied by action, is dead.** (James 2:14-17).

> [26] **As the body without the spirit is dead, so faith without deeds is dead.** (James 2:26).

The Holy Spirit and Discernment

We look to the Spirit not only to show us the truth but also to point out what is not truth. Everyone is exposed to much that is false in this world, and Christians are no exception. In fact, there are so many false teachers and so much false doctrine in the marketplace that Christians really have to be careful not to be taken in. Scripture warns us about this and tells us to test the spirits to discern if they are true or false.

> [1] **Dear friends, do not believe every spirit, but test the spirits to see whether they are from God, because many false prophets have gone out into the world.** (1 John 4:1).

> [29] **I know that after I leave, savage wolves will come in among you and will not spare the flock.** [30] **Even from your own number men will arise and distort the truth in order to draw away disciples after them.** (Acts 20:29-30).

If we are to discern the spirits, we certainly cannot depend on our sinful human nature to do it. It could not do it before we were saved, and it cannot do it after we are saved. No, we must look to the Holy Spirit for discernment, and ask Him to show us what is true and what is false.

Overcoming Sin by The Holy Spirit

The lure of sin is often so strong that man will pursue it even when his conscience loudly proclaims that it is wrong and warns him of the high cost. For most people, the temptation to sin is even greater if they think they can conceal the sin. Often, if the sin is hidden from man the sinner seems to think it is hidden from God. Sin that is done in secret may be punished out in the open. This happened to David.

[11] "This is what the LORD says: 'Out of your own household I am going to bring calamity upon you. Before your very eyes I will take your wives and give them to one who is close to you, and he will lie with your wives in broad daylight. [12] You did it in secret, but I will do this thing in broad daylight before all Israel.'" (2 Samuel 12:11-12).

In one of his Psalms, David tells of his unbearable guilt over unconfessed sin and his relief when he finally confessed.

[3] When I kept silent, my bones wasted away through my groaning all day long. [4] For day and night your hand was heavy upon me; my strength was sapped as in the heat of summer. [5] Then I acknowledged my sin to you and did not cover up my iniquity. I said, "I will confess my transgressions to the LORD"— and you forgave the guilt of my sin. (Psalm 32:3-5).

The pull of sin on the Christian can only be effectively overcome by the control of the Holy Spirit. Being controlled by the Spirit does away with the desire we have to sin because the Spirit hates sin. Christians who fail to make being controlled by the Spirit a way of life find themselves making numerous attempts to subdue their sinful natures and conquer sin. Sometimes they attain a high degree of success for a brief period, only to fall back again into their old ways.

Scripture teaches and experience proves that the believer, in his own strength, is unable to live the Christian life called for in the Bible. He must look to the indwelling Sprit to enable and empower him.

If we are serious about not wanting to sin, we will ask God for the strength to resist it. The more time we spend asking God to keep us from sin, the less time we spend asking God to forgive sin. Submitting to the control of the Holy Spirit will lead to spiritual growth and strength, because He will apply the means of grace to us and bring it about.

The new Christian, as well as the Christian of many years, can be controlled by the Spirit. Being controlled is not based on how long one has been a Christian or how much one knows about the Bible. It is based solely on being yielded to the Spirit. As we yield to Him, He will lead us and teach us so that we begin to mature in the faith. He gives us a closer walk with God. The closer we walk with God, the more sensitive we become to sin — both in the knowledge of it and the hatred of it. Also, we are more prepared to do battle with the spiritual powers that we face. And we do face spiritual powers. We must not forget for a moment that we are truly in a spiritual war. Paul tells us that in Ephesians 6:10-12.

> [10] Finally, be strong in the Lord and in his mighty power. [11] Put on the full armor of God so that you can take your stand against the devil's schemes. [12] For our struggle is not against flesh and blood, but against the rulers, against the authorities, against the powers of this dark world and against the spiritual forces of evil in the heavenly realms. (Ephesians 6:10-12).

We need to be aware that the span of time between when we are saved and when we die physically is a spiritual battlefield. Satan hates God, and he tries to get at God through God's people. He and his demons will do all they can to keep people from trusting Christ. They will try to get those who do trust Christ to change their minds and to turn away from Christ. When all else fails they will try to keep the Christian from being effective and doing God's work. They lure and tempt the Christian to sin.

> [4] The god of this age has blinded the minds of unbelievers, so that they cannot see the light of the gospel of the glory of Christ, who is the image of God. (2 Corinthians 4:4).

> [24] And the Lord's servant must not quarrel; instead, he must be kind to everyone, able to teach, not

resentful. [25] Those who oppose him he must gently instruct, in the hope that God will grant them repentance leading them to a knowledge of the truth, [26] and that they will come to their senses and escape from the trap of the devil, who has taken them captive to do his will. (2 Timothy 2:24-26).

[8] Be self-controlled and alert. Your enemy the devil prowls around like a roaring lion looking for someone to devour. (1 Peter 5:8).

In our spiritual war we do not want to underestimate the strength of our enemy. We are no match for any of the evil spirits. The Apostle Paul had planned on going to Thessalonica but Satan was able to stop him.

[17] But, brothers, when we were torn away from you for a short time (in person, not in thought), out of our intense longing we made every effort to see you. [18] For we wanted to come to you—certainly I, Paul, did, again and again—but Satan stopped us. (1 Thessalonians 2:17-18).

As we face temptations or problems that Satan puts before us, let us remember that we need to face them in God's strength — not our own. Let us face them in faith and in submission to God's Holy Spirit. By His grace and in His strength we can then resist Satan.

[16] In addition to all this, take up the shield of faith, with which you can extinguish all the flaming arrows of the evil one. (Ephesians 6:16).

[7] Submit yourselves, then, to God. Resist the devil, and he will flee from you. (James 4:7).

Being in a spiritual war and having to fight our way across the span of time to reach our objective — heaven — can be a real struggle. We can grow weary; however, we can't quit. If we do, we will never reach our objective.

[12] Because of the increase of wickedness, the love of most will grow cold, [13] but he who stands firm to the end will be saved. (Matthew 24:12-13).

Paul knew first hand what a struggle the Christian life is, and he encouraged Timothy to fight.

[18] **Timothy, my son, I give you this instruction in keeping with the prophecies once made about you, so that by following them you may fight the good fight...** (1 Timothy 1:18).

[3] **Endure hardship with us like a good soldier of Christ Jesus.** (2 Timothy 2:3).

However, Paul did not ask Timothy to do anything that he himself did not do. Paul had fought the same enemies we fight — the world, the flesh, and the devil. And by the grace of God he had kept the faith.

[7] **I have fought the good fight, I have finished the race, I have kept the faith.** (2 Timothy 4:7).

Those who fight this war are those that love Christ. They demonstrate that love by striving to obey Christ's commands. There are others who profess Christ, and they "put on a good show" for their fellow man, but they don't obey Christ's commands — they don't truly love Him. Christ lets them know that they don't belong to Him.

[21] **"Not everyone who says to me, 'Lord, Lord,' will enter the kingdom of heaven, but only he who does the will of my Father who is in heaven.** [22] **Many will say to me on that day, 'Lord, Lord, did we not prophesy in your name, and in your name drive out demons and perform many miracles?'** [23] **Then I will tell them plainly, 'I never knew you. Away from me, you evildoers!'** (Matthew 7:21-23).

[22] **Then Jesus went through the towns and villages, teaching as he made his way to Jerusalem.** [23] **Someone asked him, "Lord, are only a few people going to be saved?" He said to them,** [24] **"Make every effort to enter through the narrow door, because many, I tell you, will try to enter and will not be able to.** [25] **Once the owner of the house gets up and**

> closes the door, you will stand outside knocking and
> pleading, 'Sir, open the door for us.' "But he will
> answer, 'I don't know you or where you come from.'
> ²⁶ "Then you will say, 'We ate and drank with you,
> and you taught in our streets.' ²⁷ "But he will reply, 'I
> don't know you or where you come from. Away from
> me, all you evildoers!' (Luke 13:22-27).

Scripture is clear, a heart that loves Christ is a heart
that seeks to obey Christ. However, in trying to be obedient
we do a better job of abstaining from sinful acts than we do
in performing good deeds. Many Christians don't realize that
failing to do the good that God calls us to do is a sin, but
God's Word says it is.

> ¹⁷ Anyone, then, who knows the good he ought to do
> and doesn't do it, sins. (James 4:17).

As we bring this discussion of sin and spiritual warfare
to a close, let us resolve to renew our efforts, work harder,
and keep pushing toward our objective, until by force we lay
hold of it.

> ¹² From the days of John the Baptist until now, the
> kingdom of heaven has been forcefully advancing,
> and forceful men lay hold of it. (Matthew 11:12).

We don't want to forget where our strength to fight this
war comes from. Let us seek to be led and empowered by
God's Holy Spirit. When we are empowered by the Spirit, He
will give us the strength with which to fight.

> ¹³ I can do everything through him who gives me
> strength. (Philippians 4:13).

In this spiritual war we may not be able to see Satan
and his demons, but they are as real as anything we can
see. They are powerful and very destructive. The only way
we can fight against spiritual power is with spiritual power.
As we fight our battles in the power of the Holy Spirit, we can
be confident of victory.

⁴ You, dear children, are from God and have overcome them, because the one who is in you is greater than the one who is in the world. (1 John 4:4).

The Holy Spirit and The Church

The Holy Spirit works in each believer to bring about God's purpose for that person's life. He works through the combined lives of all believers to bring about His purpose for His church. He works to build, encourage, and strengthen the church.

³¹ Then the church throughout Judea, Galilee and Samaria enjoyed a time of peace. It was strengthened; and encouraged by the Holy Spirit, it grew in numbers, living in the fear of the Lord. (Acts 9:31).

God's church is the invisible church. It is made up of those whom God indwells by His Holy Spirit. There is also the visible church. The visible church is comprised of the many churches and denominations around the world that meet on Sunday morning to worship God. However, so much of this worship is not pleasing to God. Often it is done by people who don't know God. In addition, many who do know God, don't know how to worship Him according to Scripture. Christ tells us that God is to be worshipped in spirit and in truth.

²³ Yet a time is coming and has now come when the true worshipers will worship the Father in spirit and truth, for they are the kind of worshipers the Father seeks. ²⁴ God is spirit, and his worshipers must worship in spirit and in truth." (John 4:23-24).

We learn what the truth is when we look to the Holy Spirit to teach us as we study God's Word, and hear the Word preached.

¹³ But when he, the Spirit of truth, comes, he will guide you into all truth. He will not speak on his

> own; he will speak only what he hears, and he will
> tell you what is yet to come. (John 16:13).

We worship in spirit when we are controlled by the Holy Spirit. He is the one who will give us the right attitude of heart as we sing hymns, pray, listen to the sermon, and fellowship with other believers.

> [3] For it is we who are the circumcision, we who worship by the Spirit of God, who glory in Christ Jesus, and who put no confidence in the flesh... (Philippians 3:3).

The visible church includes all of those who are on a church membership role or who attend a church. The invisible church is part of the visible church. It is the true church within the visible church that the world sees. Only God knows for sure who are members of the invisible church. There are some who may be Christians but they don't act like they are. On the other hand they may not even be Christians. Diotrephes seems to be one of these.

> [9] I wrote to the church, but Diotrephes, who loves to be first, will have nothing to do with us. [10] So if I come, I will call attention to what he is doing, gossiping maliciously about us. Not satisfied with that, he refuses to welcome the brothers. He also stops those who want to do so and puts them out of the church. (3 John 9-10).

We know from Scripture and from experience that all who are in the visible church are not in the invisible church. There are those in the visible church who are not Christians — they do not have the Holy Spirit. Sometimes these men are in positions of authority as leaders or officers in the church.

> [12] These men are blemishes at your love feasts, eating with you without the slightest qualm— shepherds who feed only themselves. They are

clouds without rain, blown along by the wind; autumn trees, without fruit and uprooted—twice dead. [16] These men are grumblers and faultfinders; they follow their own evil desires; they boast about themselves and flatter others for their own advantage. [17] But, dear friends, remember what the apostles of our Lord Jesus Christ foretold. [18] They said to you, "In the last times there will be scoffers who will follow their own ungodly desires." [19] These are the men who divide you, who follow mere natural instincts and do not have the Spirit.
(Jude 12, 16-19).

Those indwelt by God's Holy Spirit comprise His temple. We know that God is everywhere; however, the temple of God is His earthly dwelling place. In the Old Testament, it was a physical building with physical properties that was made by hands. Since the Cross, the temple of God is a spiritual building with spiritual properties made without hands. Being indwelt by God, there is a sense in which each believer and each local congregation of believers is a temple of God. However, collectively, Christians are the temple of God. As believers, we are all building blocks in God's temple — living stones in a living building.

[16] What agreement is there between the temple of God and idols? For we are the temple of the living God. As God has said: "I will live with them and walk among them, and I will be their God, and they will be my people."
(2 Corinthians 6:16).

[19] Consequently, you are no longer foreigners and aliens, but fellow citizens with God's people and members of God's household, [20] built on the foundation of the apostles and prophets, with Christ Jesus himself as the chief cornerstone. [21] In him the whole building is joined together and rises to become a holy temple in the Lord. [22] And in him you too are being built together to become a dwelling in which God lives by his Spirit. (Ephesians 2:19-22).

[16] Don't you know that you yourselves are God's temple and that God's Spirit lives in you? (1 Corinthians 3:16).

⁴ As you come to him, the living Stone—rejected by men but chosen by God and precious to him—⁵ you also, like living stones, are being built into a spiritual house to be a holy priesthood, offering spiritual sacrifices acceptable to God through Jesus Christ. (1 Peter 2:4-5).

Unity in The Holy Spirit

As we are living stones in a living building, we must remember that this is not just any old building, and we are not just any old stones put in any old place. This building is designed by God. We are stones that are chosen by God. Our place in the building is determined by God. The Holy Spirit works to shape us so that we fit into our particular place. Often, the shaping process requires a good bit of cutting, chiseling, and grinding. It can be painful at times. However, it is necessary in order that we fit properly into our place. As each of us is made to fit, there is a unity that makes for strength. This unity is in the Holy Spirit. It is given to us by the Holy Spirit, and we are to make every effort to keep it.

³ Make every effort to keep the unity of the Spirit through the bond of peace. (Ephesians 4:3).

This unity is not external. It does not mean that all of us are to do the same thing, or do things the same way. It is not a unity in the method or mode of our worship. It is a unity of spirit produced by the Holy Spirit. It is a oneness with God and, through God, a oneness with each other. We have the same God as our Father, the same Christ as our Savior, and the same Spirit as our Counselor. The same Spirit has renewed us and imparted faith to us. We are all members of the same body — the body of Christ. We are all servants of the same master, soldiers in the same army, and live for the same purpose — to glorify God.

When we think of the different temperaments of man, the different backgrounds he comes from, and the different cultures he lives in, we realize that only the Holy Spirit can maintain our unity. However, it is up to each of us to yield to Him in order for this to be done. We are to do our best to keep the unity. We do this through the bond of peace. Having made peace with God through Jesus Christ, we remain at peace with God through obedience. If we are at peace with God, then we will be at peace with each other. This peace is more than an absence of conflict. It springs from an internal spirit of love that is expressed in outward acts of love.

Our Home and The Holy Spirit

Think what it would be like if Christians continually exemplified Christian love. Think of the decrease in conflicts, arguments, and other acts of sin that would take place. It is so much easier not to sin when in the company of believers who have their hearts and minds on God. Most of us have been to a Christian gathering or retreat where everyone professed to know Christ, where there were sermons and teachings about Christ, and the music and conversation was centered on Christ. In this environment it was much easier to show love to others and to be at peace with others. There was less temptation to sin, and it was easier to resist sin than it is in the atmosphere of the everyday world.

That being the case, think what it would be like to have a truly Christ-centered home. I say "truly" because too often the term "Christ-centered" means nothing more than those living there have accepted Christ. They may be in Christ, but they are not living for Christ. Most of the time, neither their home nor their lives are under the control of the Holy Spirit — they are under the control of the flesh. The Apostle Paul gave the Colossian Christians some guidelines for holy living. Wouldn't it be wonderful if everyone in our homes practiced these guidelines? It can only be done under the control of the Holy Spirit.

> [12] Therefore, as God's chosen people, holy and dearly loved, clothe yourselves with compassion, kindness, humility, gentleness and patience. [13] Bear with each other and forgive whatever grievances you may have against one another. Forgive as the Lord forgave you. [14] And over all these virtues put on love, which binds them all together in perfect unity. (Colossians 3:12-14).

Just think what a home could be like if everyone in it got serious about their Christian commitment. For husbands, wives, parents and children, a good place to start is God's commands in Ephesians.

> [22] Wives, submit to your husbands as to the Lord. [23] For the husband is the head of the wife as Christ is the head of the church, his body, of which he is the Savior. [24] Now as the church submits to Christ, so also wives should submit to their husbands in everything. [25] Husbands, love your wives, just as Christ loved the church and gave himself up for her [26] to make her holy, cleansing her by the washing with water through the word, [27] and to present her to himself as a radiant church, without stain or wrinkle or any other blemish, but holy and blameless. [28] In this same way, husbands ought to love their wives as their own bodies. He who loves his wife loves himself. [29] After all, no one ever hated his own body, but he feeds and cares for it, just as Christ does the church—[30] for we are members of his body. [31] "For this reason a man will leave his father and mother and be united to his wife, and the two will become one flesh." [32] This is a profound mystery—but I am talking about Christ and the church.
> (Ephesians 5:22-32).

> [1] Children, obey your parents in the Lord, for this is right. [2] "Honor your father and mother"—which is the first commandment with a promise—[3] "that it may go well with you and that you may enjoy long life on the earth." [4] Fathers, do not exasperate your children; instead, bring them up in the training and instruction of the Lord. (Ephesians 6:1-4).

In any home, there is unlimited potential for a committed believer to be used by the Holy Spirit to bring about love, joy, and peace. Each of us needs to ask: Am I that committed believer? Am I being used by the Holy Spirit to make it easier for others in my home to maintain a close walk with God? If not, why not?

Problem of Surrendering to The Holy Spirit

Surrendering our lives totally to the control of the Holy Spirit is easier said than done. Our human nature rebels at the thought of someone else controlling us — using us to do their work in order to accomplish their purpose. We all have a desire to do our own thing. We want to feel free and be free to do what pleases us. To deny ourselves and surrender it all is a big step.

Often the thoughts that cause us to hesitate to give up control of our lives to the Holy Spirit are questions such as: What will He want me to be? What will He want me to do? Where will He want me to go? Not knowing the answers, some Christians are afraid to surrender their lives totally for fear that God will take advantage of them, and they will have to do what they do not want to do. They fear that God will send them to their "Nineveh." (Read the Book of Jonah in the Old Testament of the Bible.)

That being the case, they should first realize that, like Jonah, they are sinning by trying to avoid doing God's will. Secondly, God can get them to their "Nineveh" the hard way, just as He did Jonah. Thirdly, they fail to understand that once we have given the Holy Spirit complete control of our life, we want to do what He wants us to do. We put aside our will and seek to do His will. It becomes a privilege to have His commands and a blessing to obey them. It is in our obedience that we experience His peace and joy.

A subtle and self-deceiving substitute for turning our lives over to the Holy Spirit is the giving of material things.

For most Christians, it is easier to surrender <u>things</u> to God than it is to surrender <u>oneself</u>. Christians can give possessions and money, even tithe, without giving themselves to the control of the Holy Spirit. Some will give their time but they are not willing to surrender a particular sin. Christians should be aware of the fact that the time we spend not living under the control of the Holy Spirit is time spent in sin. Moreover, it shows that we either have forgotten or are not concerned that we are called to live our lives for Christ who died for us.

> [15] **And he died for all, that those who live should no longer live for themselves but for him who died for them and was raised again.** (2 Corinthians 5:15).

Drawn Closer in Suffering

There is one thing that causes most Christians to seek to draw closer to God — suffering. It is in our trials and suffering that we are more ready to listen to Him and to obey Him. Until troubles come, some Christians seem to think of God as being in heaven far removed from them, as opposed to the reality that He is right there with them and in them. They spend little time thinking of Him and less time in communion with Him. As long as their health is good, their finances fine, and their loved ones are okay, they live as though their purpose in life is to seek to be happy rather than to glorify God. But when troubles come they turn to Him and acknowledge their sinful ways. Sometimes they will promise to do better if God will just solve the problem they are experiencing. God is sovereign and He may or may not solve their problem for them depending on what He knows is best. However, because He is faithful they will find the comfort of His presence with them.

> [9] **If we confess our sins, he is faithful and just and will forgive us our sins and purify us from all unrighteousness.** (1 John 1:9).

[13...] **if we are faithless, he will remain faithful, for he cannot disown himself.** (2 Timothy 2:13).

You are forgiving and good, O Lord, abounding in love to all who call to you. [6] **Hear my prayer, O LORD; listen to my cry for mercy.** [7] **In the day of my trouble I will call to you, for you will answer me.**
(Psalm 86:5-7).

How wonderful it is to know that God remains faithful. The most faithful of men are subject to moments of unfaithfulness, but God is eternally faithful. However, let us not be presumptuous about God's faithfulness. It is unrealistic to think that we can make it a habit to live for ourselves in good times, and seek to draw close to God only in times of trouble. We cannot profess Christ with our lips but deny Him in our hearts and by our deeds. That would be mockery, and God will not be mocked.

[9] **Fools mock at making amends for sin, but goodwill is found among the upright.** (Proverbs 14:9).

[7] **Do not be deceived: God cannot be mocked. A man reaps what he sows.** [8] **The one who sows to please his sinful nature, from that nature will reap destruction; the one who sows to please the Spirit, from the Spirit will reap eternal life.** (Galatians 6:7-8).

Professing Christ but living for self is deceiving, and the one doing this will reap destruction. Paul says it brings spiritual death.

[12] **Therefore, brothers, we have an obligation—but it is not to the sinful nature, to live according to it.** [13] **For if you live according to the sinful nature, you will die; but if by the Spirit you put to death the misdeeds of the body, you will live...**
(Romans 8:12-13).

The degree to which one lives for the flesh is the degree to which one endangers the soul. Notice in verse 12 that this is addressed to brothers — those professing Christ. However, the statement Paul makes is without exception. "If you live according to the sinful nature, you will die."

All through Scripture we see that true faith, producing a true profession, is expected to result in obedience. And it will. Although it will not be perfect, it will be a trend toward obedience. The true professor will not just intend to be obedient, but he will <u>strive</u> to be obedient. We know that Scripture teaches that the saved love Christ, and that those who love Christ obey His commands. Therefore, we are left with only one conclusion concerning those who profess but do not truly seek to obey His commands — they are not saved. They do not love Christ. He says that if they did, they would obey His commands.

> [15] **"If you love me, you will obey what I command.**
> (John 14:15).

Remember, our works do not save us, and we are not kept saved by our works. However, we are to be busy working because we are saved. We are to do God's work to God's glory. Never let the fact of our being saved by grace cause us to rationalize away the need for us to work. In other words, don't not work because you or someone else might think you are trying to be saved or stay saved by working. Be confident of the fact that you are saved by grace.

> [8] **For it is by grace you have been saved, through faith—and this not from yourselves, it is the gift of God—[9] not by works, so that no one can boast.**
> (Ephesians 2:8-9).

Once you have been saved by grace, then be confident of the fact that you were saved to do good works. You are to produce fruit.

> [8] **This is to my Father's glory, that you bear much fruit, showing yourselves to be my disciples.**
> (John 15:8).

A Christian is called to live 24 hours a day, seven days a week to glorify God. Are you doing that? You were bought with a price — the shed blood of Jesus Christ. You are now a slave to God.

> **[22] But now that you have been set free from sin and have become slaves to God, the benefit you reap leads to holiness, and the result is eternal life.** (Romans 6:22).

You have no time of your own. You have no rights of your own. Your life is to be lived for the purpose of glorifying God.

> **[31] So whether you eat or drink or whatever you do, do it all for the glory of God.** (1 Corinthians 10:31).

This is the teaching throughout Scripture. We must do more than just taste of the Holy Spirit. We must live and work in obedience to Him, showing that we possess Him and that He possesses us. We can only do this in His power. However, we are not to just sit in our easy chair and expect the Spirit to do good works through us. The grace of the Spirit is not an excuse for us to shirk our responsibility. His working does not reduce the need for us to work but rather it increases it. We must work to give expression to the Spirit's work — both in us and through us. We are to actively seek His will; moreover, we are to carry it out under His direction and in His strength. Then the work we do becomes work that will stand the test of fire.

> **[13...]his work will be shown for what it is, because the Day will bring it to light. It will be revealed with fire, and the fire will test the quality of each man's work.** (1 Corinthians 3:13).

Of course, there are many Christians who walk close to God most of the time, not just when they are troubled. They experience the blessings of peace and joy that come as a result of obedience. Also, because they are obedient they can have confidence that when trials come into their lives, they are not there for disciplinary reasons.

It is the common lot of all men in this fallen and corrupt world to undergo some degree of trials and suffering. However, no one has ever suffered or will ever suffer as our Lord Jesus Christ did. He suffered trials and the temptations of the world, while at the same time undergoing persecution and rejection by the world. He, who committed no sin, suffered and paid the penalty for the sins of others. We cannot even begin to imagine how awful His suffering was, but He knew what He faced. Knowing what was ahead of Him, His human nature was reluctant but compliant. He was stressed and wanted to avoid the tremendous suffering that lay ahead. However, He came for that purpose — to suffer in our place and pay the penalty for our sins. As the God-man, He would let nothing stop Him. In obedience to the Father and in the power of the Holy Spirit, He willingly went to the cross.

[32] They went to a place called Gethsemane, and Jesus said to his disciples, "Sit here while I pray." [33] He took Peter, James and John along with him, and he began to be deeply distressed and troubled. [34] "My soul is overwhelmed with sorrow to the point of death," he said to them. "Stay here and keep watch." [35] Going a little farther, he fell to the ground and prayed that if possible the hour might pass from him. [36] "*Abba*, Father," he said, "everything is possible for you. Take this cup from me. Yet not what I will, but what you will." (Mark 14:32-36).

[41] He withdrew about a stone's throw beyond them, knelt down and prayed, [42] "Father, if you are willing, take this cup from me; yet not my will, but yours be done." [43] An angel from heaven appeared to him and strengthened him. [44] And being in anguish, he prayed more earnestly, and his sweat was like drops of blood falling to the ground. (Luke 22:41-44).

[7] During the days of Jesus' life on earth, he offered up prayers and petitions with loud cries and tears to the one who could save him from death, and he was heard because of his reverent submission. [8] Although he was a son, he learned obedience from what he suffered... (Hebrews 5:7-8).

We read above in Hebrews 5:8 that Jesus learned obedience from what He suffered. Because this verse can be confusing let us look closer at what is being said here. Jesus was sinless. He never disobeyed, so there was not a need to learn to obey. The obedience He learned was <u>not how to be obedient</u> but <u>what it was like to be obedient</u>. He experienced what it takes to live under trials and temptations and through it all to remain obedient and not sin. He experienced how tough it was to suffer and die on the cross. He experienced what it was to be forsaken by God. The obedience of Jesus was experiential.

We read above in Luke 22:43 that an angel strengthened Jesus. Being man, Jesus suffered as a man, and His heavenly Father sent an angel to strengthen Him. This same heavenly Father is our Father, and He will also strengthen us in our time of need.

> [1] **God is our refuge and strength, an ever-present help in trouble.** (Psalm 46:1b).

> [16] **I pray that out of his glorious riches he may strengthen you with power through his Spirit in your inner being...** (Ephesians 3:16).

> [10] **So do not fear, for I am with you; do not be dismayed, for I am your God. I will strengthen you and help you; I will uphold you with my righteous right hand.** (Isaiah 41:10).

> [7] **The LORD is good, a refuge in times of trouble. He cares for those who trust in him...** (Nahum 1:7).

> [3] **He heals the brokenhearted and binds up their wounds.** (Psalm 147:3).

The Scriptures never tell us that we will not suffer; rather they make it clear that we will. Moreover, they are not as concerned with our being relieved of our suffering as they are with how well we bear up under it. We know that God is working everything for our good.

> [28] And we know that in all things God works for the good of those who love him, who have been called according to his purpose. (Romans 8:28).

And this includes our suffering. We are to glorify God not only in our easier times but also in the times of trials. It is in the times of trials that we find out how much faith we have and how strongly we are committed. Through trials we develop perseverance.

> [10] If you falter in times of trouble, how small is your strength! (Proverbs 24:10).

> [8] We are hard pressed on every side, but not crushed; perplexed, but not in despair; [9] persecuted, but not abandoned; struck down, but not destroyed. (2 Corinthians 4:8-9).

> [3]...because you know that the testing of your faith develops perseverance. (James 1:3).

Being persecuted because of our stand for Christ is a form of suffering and trial that all Christians undergo. When we are persecuted for Christ's sake we are told to rejoice. We do not rejoice because of the suffering itself but because it is due to our identity with Christ. Our confidence that we belong to Him is strengthened, and we can rejoice knowing that we will one day be rewarded by going to be with Him.

> [12] Dear friends, do not be surprised at the painful trial you are suffering, as though something strange were happening to you. [13] But rejoice that you participate in the sufferings of Christ, so that you may be overjoyed when his glory is revealed. [14] If you are insulted because of the name of Christ, you are blessed, for the Spirit of glory and of God rests on you. [15] If you suffer, it should not be as a murderer or thief or any other kind of criminal, or even as a meddler. [16] However, if you suffer as a Christian, do not be ashamed, but praise God that you bear that name. [17] For it is time for judgment to begin with the family of God; and if it begins with us, what will the outcome be for those who do not obey the gospel of God? (1 Peter 4:12-17).

> [11] "Blessed are you when people insult you, persecute you and falsely say all kinds of evil against you because of me. [12] Rejoice and be glad, because great is your reward in heaven, for in the same way they persecuted the prophets who were before you. (Matthew 5:11-12).

> [40] His speech persuaded them. They called the apostles in and had them flogged. Then they ordered them not to speak in the name of Jesus, and let them go. [41] The apostles left the Sanhedrin, rejoicing because they had been counted worthy of suffering disgrace for the Name. [42] Day after day, in the temple courts and from house to house, they never stopped teaching and proclaiming the good news that Jesus is the Christ. (Acts 5:40-42).

Christians need to be on guard against Satan at all times, but particularly during a time of suffering. Many of our troubles originate with Satan, but he will also attempt to use to his advantage those troubles that do not. If he can catch us in a weakened condition with our guard down, he may get us engulfed in sin.

James tells us to resist the devil. How do we do that? Knowing what we do about the devil's power, surely no human thinks of himself as his equal. The only way we can resist him is in God's power.

> [7] Submit yourselves, then, to God. Resist the devil, and he will flee from you. (James 4:7).

The more we submit to God, the easier it will be to resist the devil. As we humble ourselves and seek to do God's will, He gives us the necessary grace with which to do it.

> [6] But he gives us more grace. That is why Scripture says: "God opposes the proud but gives grace to the humble." (James 4:6).

We see God's grace at work in the lives of some Christians who suffer much more than most of us ever will.

Yet, in His grace they are strengthened as they accept His will for their lives. They can even pray that He will glorify Himself in their suffering. This cannot be done in the flesh. It takes the enabling of the Holy Spirit to pray this way. We should thank God for these people and for the example of faith they set for us. It is an encouragement to us to see what God has done in their lives — the peace and joy He has given them in their adversity, and the way He has sustained them. It gives us hope that if we find ourselves in a similar situation He will do the same for us. God uses their example of faith to strengthen us.

Paul thanked God for the Thessalonian Christians whose faith and love were increasing under persecution and trials.

> [3] **We ought always to thank God for you, brothers, and rightly so, because your faith is growing more and more, and the love every one of you has for each other is increasing.** [4] **Therefore, among God's churches we boast about your perseverance and faith in all the persecutions and trials you are enduring.** [5] **All this is evidence that God's judgment is right, and as a result you will be counted worthy of the kingdom of God, for which you are suffering.**
> (2 Thessalonians 1:3-5).

The Holy Spirit will always supply the grace we need to accomplish the task He has laid before us. This is also true in our suffering. If our suffering becomes more severe, He supplies us with more grace. We are as dependent on God for the increase of grace as we are when we first receive grace. It is comforting to know that our suffering is not for naught, but that God makes it work for our good and for the good of others. He uses it to draw us closer to Himself, to strengthen our faith, to make us more like Christ, and to give us a firmer hope of heaven.

> [67] **Before I was afflicted I went astray, but now I obey your word.** [71] **It was good for me to be afflicted so that I might learn your decrees.** (Psalm 119:67, 71).

[3] Not only so, but we also rejoice in our sufferings, because we know that suffering produces perseverance; [4] perseverance, character; and character, hope. [5] And hope does not disappoint us, because God has poured out his love into our hearts by the Holy Spirit, whom he has given us. (Romans 5:3-5).

[50] My comfort in my suffering is this: Your promise preserves my life. (Psalm 119:50).

[28] And we know that in all things God works for the good of those who love him, who have been called according to his purpose. [29] For those God foreknew he also predestined to be conformed to the likeness of his Son, that he might be the firstborn among many brothers. [30] And those he predestined, he also called; those he called, he also justified; those he justified, he also glorified. (Romans 8:28-30).

Christian Works and The Holy Spirit

Another important reason why the Christian needs to understand the work of the Holy Spirit and to let Him control his life is that the Spirit knows the work the Christian is to do. Not only does the Spirit know the work we are to do, but He also knows when we are to do it and how we are to do it. In addition to leading us, the Spirit will open and close doors so that the circumstances involving our work will fit with what we are doing. We need to obey the leading of the Spirit in order to accomplish what we are called to do. Are we doing that? Philip, Peter, and Paul are three examples of men who did.

[29] The Spirit told Philip, "Go to that chariot and stay near it." [30] Then Philip ran up to the chariot and heard the man reading Isaiah the prophet. "Do you understand what you are reading?" Philip asked. [31] "How can I," he said, "unless someone explains it to me?" So he invited Philip to come up and sit with him. [32] The eunuch was reading this passage of Scripture: "He was led like a sheep to the slaughter,

and as a lamb before the shearer is silent, so he did not open his mouth. [33] In his humiliation he was deprived of justice. Who can speak of his descendants? For his life was taken from the earth." [34] The eunuch asked Philip, "Tell me, please, who is the prophet talking about, himself or someone else?" [35] Then Philip began with that very passage of Scripture and told him the good news about Jesus. (Acts 8:29-35).

[19] While Peter was still thinking about the vision, the Spirit said to him, "Simon, three men are looking for you. [20] So get up and go downstairs. Do not hesitate to go with them, for I have sent them." [21] Peter went down and said to the men, "I'm the one you're looking for. Why have you come?" (Acts 10:19-21).

[6] Paul and his companions traveled throughout the region of Phrygia and Galatia, having been kept by the Holy Spirit from preaching the word in the province of Asia. [7] When they came to the border of Mysia, they tried to enter Bithynia, but the Spirit of Jesus would not allow them to. [8] So they passed by Mysia and went down to Troas. [9] During the night Paul had a vision of a man of Macedonia standing and begging him, "Come over to Macedonia and help us." [10] After Paul had seen the vision, we got ready at once to leave for Macedonia, concluding that God had called us to preach the gospel to them. (Acts 16:6-10).

Matthew 28:18-20 is commonly called the Great Commission. All Christians are called to help carry out the Great Commission, but where do we start? How do we know what our particular role is?

[18] Then Jesus came to them and said, "All authority in heaven and on earth has been given to me. [19] Therefore go and make disciples of all nations, baptizing them in the name of the Father and of the Son and of the Holy Spirit, [20] and teaching them to obey everything I have commanded you. And surely I am with you always, to the very end of the age." (Matthew 28:18-20).

Before the world was made, God determined what the works are that each Christian will do, and only as the Christian yields to the Holy Spirit will he know what to do.

> **10 For we are God's workmanship, created in Christ Jesus to do good works, which God prepared in advance for us to do.** (Ephesians 2:10).

We Christians need to be careful how we consider Ephesians 2:10. We are so accustomed to hearing the term work used as it relates to a job. We separate our work life from our family or home life. A certain amount of time is allotted to work, and we consider the rest of the time " our time." For the Christian there is no separation between doing good works and living the Christian life — they are one and the same. The Amplified Bible version of Ephesians 2:10 helps us to better understand this.

> **For we are God's [own] handiwork (His workmanship), recreated in Christ Jesus, [born anew] that we may do those good works which God predestined (planned beforehand) for us, (taking paths which He prepared ahead of time) that we should walk in them—living the good life which He prearranged and made ready for us to live.** (Ephesians 2:10).

Christians are called to be good and do good. The entire Christian life is to be a good work. Whether working at our jobs away from home or working at our jobs at home or just plain relaxing with family and friends, it is all to be done in service to Christ.

> **23 Whatever you do, work at it with all your heart, as working for the Lord, not for men, 24 since you know that you will receive an inheritance from the Lord as a reward. It is the Lord Christ you are serving.** (Colossians 3:23-24).

God began this good work in us by giving us salvation, and God continues this good work in our sanctification.

> **⁶ being confident of this, that he who began a good work in you will carry it on to completion until the day of Christ Jesus.** (Philippians 1:6).

Our thoughts, words, and deeds are all included in our good works. All are to be done to glorify God. Some of our works are done in public, but every bit as important are those done in private. The Holy Spirit gave us spiritual life, and He will enable us to live the life He gave us. We need to quit fighting Him and let Him control us. Then the good works that God prepared ahead of time for us to do will be done.

One of the most important works and one of the most neglected works is prayer. However, Scripture tells us to pray continually.

> **¹⁷ pray continually…** (1Thessalonians 5:17).

We need to remember that God is sovereign. Before the world was made, He decreed all that happens. He knows what is coming next in our lives, but we don't. However, we do know that what God has planned for us, and the rest of His creation, is the best thing that could happen. There is no way better than God's way. Therefore, we should not pray to change God's will; rather we should seek to pray God's will. When we pray in the name of Jesus, we are indicating that we believe Jesus wants us to have what we request. We know that when we pray according to God's will that He will answer and give us what we request.

> **¹⁴ This is the confidence we have in approaching God: that if we ask anything according to his will, he hears us. ¹⁵ And if we know that he hears us—whatever we ask—we know that we have what we asked of him.** (1 John 5:14-15).

The Holy Spirit knows what we should ask for and why we should ask for it. Therefore, we should always seek to pray in the Spirit.

> **¹⁸ And pray in the Spirit on all occasions with all kinds of prayers and requests.** (Ephesians 6:18a).

[20] **But you, dear friends, build yourselves up in your most holy faith and pray in the Holy Spirit.** (Jude 20).

Often, Christians hear it being said that they need to go to Bible study, witness, work on church committees, visit the sick, paint a widow's house, help the poor, raise funds for a paraministry, etc. All these things are considered good things to do. Now if the non-Christian undertakes to do these things, we know that as good as it seems it does not please God. It is not of faith. The same is true when the Christian does these things without seeking the guidance of the Holy Spirit or being sensitive to His leading. We are not to do the good works of our choice, but those we feel led by Him to do.

Having faith when we accept Christ is one thing, but are we not suppose to act in faith when ten years later we go full-time into a Christian ministry? Should we not be seeking God's guidance in a decision of this nature? Certainly we should. And we should also seek His guidance in decisions about which church to attend, what line of work to pursue, etc. Then why not in so-called decisions of lesser importance? Something that we think is a small matter may be very important to God — someone's eternal life may hinge on its outcome. If we look to God to lead us only in certain decisions or situations then, in essence, we determine what we will let God do and what we will do. In other words, we only look to Him for guidance some of the time and make all the other decisions in the flesh. Scripture makes it clear that what we do in the flesh is sin. All that we do is to be done in faith, and to the best of our discernment it is to be what we think God wants us to do.

[23]...**and everything that does not come from faith is sin.** (Romans 14:23b).

In the flesh, the Christian could very well go paint the widow's house while the Holy Spirit wanted him to witness to a friend. Or someone could go to Bible study when at that particular time the Holy Spirit wanted him to visit the sick. How would a Christian know what to do, when to do it, or how to do it unless the Holy Spirit directed and empowered him? It becomes more apparent that being controlled by the Spirit is not a spiritual luxury — it is a spiritual necessity.

Commanded To Be Controlled By The Spirit

The realization that we are commanded to be controlled by the Holy Spirit, and that we are in sin when we are not, gives us even more reason to be concerned with the ministry of the Holy Spirit. Let us look at the command to be filled with the Spirit in detail.

> [18] **Do not get drunk on wine, which leads to debauchery. Instead, be filled with the Spirit.** (Ephesians 5:18).

Being filled with the Holy Spirit means being controlled by Him. I do not read Greek, but from what I understand by reading those who do, there are four grammatical rules in the Greek language which lead us to four truths in this command to be filled with the Spirit.

1. The verb is in the imperative mode; it is a command similar to the command to be baptized.
2. The tense of the verb is present, and this tense in the imperative mode always represents action going on continually, not spasmodic action.
3. The verb is in the plural, making it a command to all Christians.
4. It is in the passive voice which means that the subject of the verb is inactive but is being acted upon. It is a work of God, not of man.

We are commanded by God to be controlled and to remain controlled by the Holy Spirit. That means we are to maintain a state of being controlled by the Holy Spirit. We are to be controlled by Him and we are to continue to be controlled by Him. In other words, we are to live our lives in all we think, say, and do under the control of the Holy Spirit.

We do not want to confuse being controlled by the Spirit as a need to have more of the Spirit. On the contrary, the Spirit is all-powerful God. We do not need more of Him; He needs more of us. We need to be more committed to Him, more surrendered to Him, and more submissive to Him. We need to place not only our Sunday school and church life under His control, but also our life as grandfather, grandmother, father, mother, son, daughter, husband, wife, single person, business executive, factory worker, homemaker, etc. under His control. He is to be in control of our hobbies whether it is photography, gardening, or travel, etc. We need to place our entertainment and recreational activities under Him. This includes the Internet, movies, TV, CDs we listen to and videos we watch, as well as the books and magazines we read. Our sex life is to be under His control. I mention these areas of our lives to help illustrate the fact that all aspects of our life, our total life, is to be lived under the control of the Holy Spirit 24 hours a day, every day. That is our target. None of us can hit it, but by God's grace it is what we are to strive for. Remember, we are sinning all of the time we are not being controlled by the Holy Spirit. First, we are disobeying the command to be controlled and second, we are being controlled by our sinful nature, which cannot please God.

It is sad to say, but many Christians put forth effort to obey the first part of Ephesians 5:18 (do not get drunk) but they give little, if any, thought to the second part (be filled with the Spirit). You can obey the first without obeying the second, but you cannot obey the second without obeying the first. And although it is a privilege and a blessing to be controlled by the Holy Spirit, we must never lose sight of the fact that it is our duty to be.

Being controlled by the Holy Spirit is easier said than done. Not only does the sinful nature impede it, but often we are hindered because we do not understand what it means to be controlled. However, if we consider how often we use the terms "filled with anger" or "full of hate" to describe someone who is under the influence or control of anger or hatred, then we may understand it better. The Bible speaks of sinful man as being filled with wickedness and full of envy. Those filled with wickedness are controlled by wickedness.

> [29] **They have become filled with every kind of wickedness, evil, greed and depravity. They are full of envy, murder, strife, deceit and malice.**
> (Romans 1:29).

While under the control of anger, most of us have spoken words or committed deeds that we later regretted. Violence and murder are often committed while a person is controlled by a raging jealousy or a burning desire for revenge. When controlled by anger or hatred we will do things we would not otherwise do. In the same way, when controlled by the Holy Spirit we do things we would not otherwise do. However, they are always good things — spiritual things.

As we seek to better understand how to be controlled by the Holy Spirit, we will begin to question ourselves as to our motivation for doing different things. Is it for materialistic gain, fame, power, an ego trip, or is it because, as best I can discern, the Holy Spirit is leading me to do it? We will grow more confident that it is the Holy Spirit leading as we spend more time asking Him to lead.

Some Christians may wonder if there is a difference in being full of the Spirit and being filled with the Spirit. There is no difference. To be full of the Spirit means the same thing as to be filled with the Spirit. Both denote that the person is under the control of the Holy Spirit. We have seen that Jesus lived His life under the control and in the power of the Holy Spirit. Luke 4:1 tells us that Jesus was full of the Holy Spirit. In the following verses we find that the apostles and other believers were spoken of as being either full of the Holy Spirit or filled with the Holy Spirit.

> [8] **Then Peter, filled with the Holy Spirit, said to them...** (Acts 4:8a).

[31] After they prayed, the place where they were meeting was shaken. And they were all filled with the Holy Spirit and spoke the word of God boldly. (Acts 4:31).

[55] But Stephen, full of the Holy Spirit, looked up to heaven and saw the glory of God, and Jesus standing at the right hand of God. (Acts 7:55).

[17] Then Ananias went to the house and entered it. Placing his hands on Saul, he said, "Brother Saul, the Lord—Jesus, who appeared to you on the road as you were coming here—has sent me so that you may see again and be filled with the Holy Spirit." (Acts 9:17).

[22] News of this reached the ears of the church at Jerusalem, and they sent Barnabas to Antioch. [23] When he arrived and saw the evidence of the grace of God, he was glad and encouraged them all to remain true to the Lord with all their hearts. [24] He was a good man, full of the Holy Spirit and faith, and a great number of people were brought to the Lord. (Acts 11:22-24).

[9] Then Saul, who was also called Paul, filled with the Holy Spirit, looked straight at Elymas and said... (Acts 13:9).

Professing Without Possessing The Holy Spirit

All Christians should concern themselves with living their lives under the control of the Holy Spirit. But the first concern of some who profess Christ should be the question: "Am I really indwelt by the Holy Spirit?" A real problem develops when some people who are not saved and therefore do not have the Holy Spirit, become so entwined with true Christians that they are able to talk and act as if they were Christians. They get involved in church work and even teach Sunday school, but it is all done in the flesh. Some of these may be hypocrites or con artists, but most are people who are sincere in what they believe. They think of themselves as being Christians. Like the Jews whom Paul speaks of in Romans 10:2, they have a zeal for God, but not according to knowledge.

> [1] Brothers, my heart's desire and prayer to God for the Israelites is that they may be saved. [2] For I can testify about them that they are zealous for God, but their zeal is not based on knowledge. [3] Since they did not know the righteousness that comes from God and sought to establish their own, they did not submit to God's righteousness. (Romans 10:1-3).

Like the Israelites, these sincere people are depending on their own righteousness rather than Christ's righteousness. They may believe all around the truth, but they do not believe the truth. They have never trusted in the One who is the truth. However, they appear so genuine that others accept them as Christians, and that makes it even easier for them to be self-deceived. It is sad when you realize that they seem to come so close to heaven and yet miss it. In the Parable of the Ten Virgins we see an example of this.

> [1] "At that time the kingdom of heaven will be like ten virgins who took their lamps and went out to meet the bridegroom. [2] Five of them were foolish and five were wise. [3] The foolish ones took their lamps but did not take any oil with them. [4] The wise, however, took oil in jars along with their lamps. [5] The bridegroom was a long time in coming, and they all became drowsy and fell asleep. [6] "At midnight the cry rang out: 'Here's the bridegroom! Come out to meet him!' [7] "Then all the virgins woke up and trimmed their lamps. [8] The foolish ones said to the wise, 'Give us some of your oil; our lamps are going out.' [9] "'No,' they replied, 'there may not be enough for both us and you. Instead, go to those who sell oil and buy some for yourselves.' [10] "But while they were on their way to buy the oil, the bridegroom arrived. The virgins who were ready went in with him

> to the wedding banquet. And the door was shut. [11] "Later the others also came. 'Sir! Sir!' they said. 'Open the door for us!' [12] "But he replied, 'I tell you the truth, I don't know you.' [13] "Therefore keep watch, because you do not know the day or the hour. (Matthew 25:1-13).

To help us better understand the parable, we will assume the position that is taken by most expositors. The bridegroom represents our Lord Jesus Christ, the ten virgins represent those who profess Christ, the lamps represent their professions, and the oil represents the Holy Spirit.

We see in the parable that the ten went out together. By being together and going out together it appears they shared some common interests. They certainly had in common the fact that they were going out to meet the same person — the bridegroom. It seems that night weddings were a common thing in that part of the world. Because the ten virgins were going to meet the bridegroom and accompany him to the wedding feast, they would need lamps. This is another thing they all had in common — each had her lamp. But now we come to a difference — a crucial difference. The parable tells us that the foolish virgins had lamps, but no oil. That is why they are called foolish. The wise ones not only had their lamps, but they also took jars of oil. The foolish virgins had a profession of Christ, but it was hollow and without substance. It was not a true profession; therefore, they lacked the Holy Spirit. They were unprepared to meet the bridegroom. On the other hand, the wise virgins had a genuine profession, were indwelt by the Holy Spirit, and were prepared. Those who recite the same creeds, sing the same hymns, and attend the same Bible studies often appear the same to their fellow man; however, they may be totally different in God's sight.

Demas was such a person. He worked with Paul for approximately six years and then turned back to the world.

> [14] Our dear friend Luke, the doctor, and Demas send greetings. (Colossians 4:14).

> [23] Epaphras, my fellow prisoner in Christ Jesus, sends you greetings. [24] And so do Mark, Aristarchus, Demas and Luke, my fellow workers.
> (Philemon 23-24).

> [9] Do your best to come to me quickly, [10] for Demas, because he loved this world, has deserted me and has gone to Thessalonica. (2 Timothy 4:9-10a).

Demas, in loving the world, showed his lack of love for God.

> [15] Do not love the world or anything in the world. If anyone loves the world, the love of the Father is not in him. (1 John 2:15).

Demas is a typical example of those who profess Christ for a while but turn away because they never did really possess Christ.

> [19] They went out from us, but they did not really belong to us. For if they had belonged to us, they would have remained with us; but their going showed that none of them belonged to us.
> (1 John 2:19).

Another example is Judas. He was one of the 12 apostles. He was taught by Jesus and worked with Jesus and the other apostles.

> [15] In those days Peter stood up among the believers (a group numbering about a hundred and twenty) [16] and said, "Brothers, the Scripture had to be fulfilled which the Holy Spirit spoke long ago through the mouth of David concerning Judas, who served as guide for those who arrested Jesus— [17] he was one of our number and shared in this ministry."
> (Acts 1:15-17).

When we read of people like Demas and Judas and others, it should stir up caution in us as to our walk with the Lord. Paul warns us to be careful that we don't fall.

> [12] So, if you think you are standing firm, be careful that you don't fall! (1 Corinthians 10:12).

Peter tells us what to do so that we will not fall.

> [5] For this very reason, make every effort to add to your faith goodness; and to goodness, knowledge; [6] and to knowledge, self-control; and to self-control, perseverance; and to perseverance, godliness; [7] and to godliness, brotherly kindness; and to brotherly kindness, love. [8] For if you possess these qualities in increasing measure, they will keep you from being ineffective and unproductive in your knowledge of our Lord Jesus Christ. [9] But if anyone does not have them, he is nearsighted and blind, and has forgotten that he has been cleansed from his past sins. [10] Therefore, my brothers, be all the more eager to make your calling and election sure. For if you do these things, you will never fall, [11] and you will receive a rich welcome into the eternal kingdom of our Lord and Savior Jesus Christ. (2 Peter 1:5-11).

By God's grace, the Holy Spirit is in the world contending with man and convicting the world of sin and righteousness and judgment.

> [3] Then the LORD said, "My Spirit will not contend with man forever, for he is mortal; his days will be a hundred and twenty years." (Genesis 6:3).

> [8] When he comes, he will convict the world of guilt in regard to sin and righteousness and judgment... (John 16:8).

The Bible speaks of those who have been enlightened, who have tasted the heavenly gift, who have shared in the Holy Spirit, who have tasted the goodness of the Word of God, and yet they are not truly converted.

> [4] It is impossible for those who have once been enlightened, who have tasted the heavenly gift, who have shared in the Holy Spirit, [5] who have tasted the goodness of the word of God and the powers of the coming age, [6] if they fall away, to be brought back to repentance, because to their loss they are crucifying the Son of God all over again and subjecting him to public disgrace. (Hebrews 6:4-6).

Think of the Israelites, they had seen the cloud by day and the fire by night, had been freed from bondage in Egypt, crossed the Red Sea, eaten the manna from heaven, and been taught God's Word. They had much enlightenment but look at the vast number of them who were lost!

The Jews of Christ's day had God's Word, and some of them searched the Scriptures diligently. Yet they did not receive Christ.

> [39] **You diligently study the Scriptures because you think that by them you possess eternal life. These are the Scriptures that testify about me, [40] yet you refuse to come to me to have life.** (John 5:39-40).

Being enlightened does not imply being saved. Many people are enlightened to the facts of the Gospel but do not believe its message. There are varying degrees of enlightenment among unbelievers. One of these being an unsaved seminary professor. As natural man he may have a great degree of natural enlightenment but still be unsaved.

Many people who spend time in a sound church, where there are a number of true Christians, have an opportunity to taste the heavenly gift (Christ). They also have an opportunity to share in the Holy Spirit and to taste that the Word of God is good. Just as one would taste food to see if it is good before eating it, they have an opportunity to taste Christ by hearing about Him from those in the pulpit and those in the pew. They hear about who He is, what He did, and what He does. They are in places where the Holy Spirit is working and with people whom the Holy Spirit indwells. Therefore, they share in the Holy Spirit in the sense that they see Him work, feel He is present in the group, share in His blessing of the group, and are actually influenced by Him to lead a more moral and selfless life. Upon being given a certain degree of understanding of Scripture, they taste it and see that God's Word is good. Experiencing all of this, they react and make a profession of Christ. However, their profession is based only on head knowledge, and lacks commitment. This was the case of the five foolish virgins. Also, it appears to have been the case of those whom Jesus knew did not truly believe, even though they had professed to believe.

> [23] Now while he was in Jerusalem at the Passover Feast, many people saw the miraculous signs he was doing and believed in his name. [24] But Jesus would not entrust himself to them, for he knew all men. [25] He did not need man's testimony about man, for he knew what was in a man. (John 2:23-25).

Apparently there were many who were impressed with the miracles that Jesus did and, in the flesh, they were ready to rally around His ministry. Jesus knew that they did not have faith but were caught up in the excitement of the miracles — take these away and they would leave. Man can be fickle; the cause he so fervently supports today is often forgotten tomorrow. Even true converts can begin their Christian lives with a flourish and later see their enthusiasm begin to wane.

We see that the ten virgins had a long wait, and they all fell asleep. They had been watching and waiting, but it seems the bridegroom was taking longer than they had expected. At midnight, they were awakened by a cry that the bridegroom was coming, and they all lit their lamps. However, the foolish virgins had failed to bring oil, and a wick burning without oil soon goes out. They now realized they were unprepared to meet the bridegroom. Being prepared involves more than getting prepared — it indicates a state of preparedness, one of staying prepared.

The foolish virgins wanted the wise ones to give them some of their oil, but the wise ones had only enough for themselves. Man cannot give the Holy Spirit — only God can. The wise virgins told the foolish to go buy oil. (The foolish virgins would not need money if they went to the right source to buy oil).

> [1] "Come, all you who are thirsty, come to the waters; and you who have no money, come, buy and eat! Come, buy wine and milk without money and without cost. (Isaiah 55:1).

However, while they were on their way to buy oil the bridegroom arrived. The virgins who were prepared went in with him to the wedding banquet, and the door was shut. When the foolish virgins returned, they asked the bridegroom to open the door; however, he told them he did not know them. Many people think that no one will be excluded from the banquet, but the parable makes it clear that some will be excluded. While the door is open, mercy and forgiveness may be found; however, once the door is closed, the time of mercy and forgiveness is past, and judgment is at hand. When Christ returns, we will not only be concerned that we have our lamps but that we also have oil for them. For it is only by the indwelling Holy Spirit that our lamps will continue to burn, and that we will be prepared to meet Him.

The Fruit of The Spirit

The term "fruit of the Spirit" is confusing to some people because they mistake it for the fruit of the Christian's life or the gifts of the Spirit. It is neither. The fruit of the Christian's life consists of those things done by the Christian. It is true that for these things to be pleasing to God, they must be done at the direction and in the power of the Holy Spirit. However, they are still done by the Christian and are fruit of the Christian's life.

The gifts of the Spirit are given to the Christian to be used for the edification of the church, and to convert people to Christ. They are gifts that are given in order to enable the Christian to do things that are fruitful in God's service. They are gifts from the Spirit, but are not to be confused with the fruit of the Spirit.

In order to make a practical distinction between the fruit of the Spirit, the fruit of the Christian's life, and the gifts of the Spirit, let us use as an example a Bible teacher. The teacher feels led of the Holy Spirit to conduct a Bible study with some fellow Christians, and in obedience, he does so.

The act of obedience in holding the study is fruit of the teacher's life. Let us assume that he is such a good teacher that it seems he has a gift for teaching. We might say he has been given the gift of teaching as a gift of the Spirit. When he is teaching the class, things come up from time to time that show the teacher to be a very kind person. We might say he manifests the virtue of kindness as fruit of the Spirit.

The fruit of the Spirit is work done within us by the Spirit. This work by the Spirit produces a character change within the Christian. As our character determines our deeds, we associate the fruit of the Spirit more with what kind of person the Christian is, rather than with what the Christian does. If we were to attempt to discern a Christian's spirituality, we would be on much safer ground to look for the fruit of the Spirit as opposed to the gifts of the Spirit.

The worldly Christian can display the use of spiritual gifts, as did those in the church at Corinth. Although all Christians do not have the same spiritual gifts, all Christians do have the same fruit of the Spirit.

> [22] **But the fruit of the Spirit is love, joy, peace, patience, kindness, goodness, faithfulness, [23] gentleness and self-control. Against such things there is no law.** (Galatians 5:22-23).

The degree to which a Christian yields to the Holy Spirit will determine the degree to which the fruit of the Spirit is manifested in his life. The only person within whom this fruit is found in perfection is Jesus Christ.

The fruit of the Spirit is not only a personal blessing to us and an enhancement to our walk with God, but it is also very much a factor in our behavior toward man, and our witness to man.

The first virtue listed as fruit of the Spirit is love. We are to love God and man.

> [37] **Jesus replied: "'Love the Lord your God with all your heart and with all your soul and with all your mind.' [38] This is the first and greatest commandment.**

> [39] And the second is like it: 'Love your neighbor as yourself.' (Matthew 22:37-39).

The love that is produced within us by the Holy Spirit is agape love (a higher love than that which is common to natural man). It is a supernatural love that comes from God.

> [7] Dear friends, let us love one another, for love comes from God. Everyone who loves has been born of God and knows God. [8] Whoever does not love does not know God, because God is love. [9] This is how God showed his love among us: He sent his one and only Son into the world that we might live through him. [10] This is love: not that we loved God, but that he loved us and sent his Son as an atoning sacrifice for our sins. [11] Dear friends, since God so loved us, we also ought to love one another. No one has ever seen God; but if we love one another God lives in us and his love is made complete in us. (1 John 4:7-12).

We see from the above verses that God is love and that He has shown us His perfect love by sending His Son to die for us. We are told that we should love one another because God loves us so much and indwells us. Actually, the only reason we can love either God or man is because God loved us first. With this being the case, if we do not love each other, something is wrong. John says our love for each other is an indication that we have been born of God.

If we have been born again, God will produce agape love within us and we will love our fellow believers. Scripture encourages us to cultivate that love so that it becomes stronger.

> [14] We know that we have passed from death to life, because we love our brothers. Anyone who does not love remains in death. (1 John 3:14).

> [22] Now that you have purified yourselves by obeying the truth so that you have sincere love for your brothers, love one another deeply, from the heart. (1 Peter 1:22).

> [9] Now about brotherly love we do not need to write to you, for you yourselves have been taught by God to love each other. (1 Thessalonians 4:9).

Although Christians are to manifest a special love for one another, they are also to show love to unbelievers. There are a number of ways that Christians do this, but none is more important than telling them about Christ: who He is, what He has done, and what He can and will do for them if they will turn to Him. However, Christian love is to go still further. We are commanded to love our enemies. Because obedience to God is the surest sign of our love for Him, if we love our enemies it should increase our confidence that we truly love God.

> [27] "But I tell you who hear me: Love your enemies, do good to those who hate you... [32] "If you love those who love you, what credit is that to you? Even 'sinners' love those who love them.
> (Luke 6:27, 32).

We see how dependent we are on God's Holy Spirit to produce love in us and enable us to show that love to others. Our dependence on the Holy Spirit is further emphasized when we seek to love as Paul defined love in 1 Corinthians.

> [1] If I speak in the tongues of men and of angels, but have not love, I am only a resounding gong or a clanging cymbal. [2] If I have the gift of prophecy and can fathom all mysteries and all knowledge, and if I have a faith that can move mountains, but have not love, I am nothing. [3] If I give all I possess to the poor and surrender my body to the flames, but have not love, I gain nothing. [4] Love is patient, love is kind. It does not envy, it does not boast, it is not proud. [5] It is not rude, it is not self-seeking, it is not easily angered, it keeps no record of wrongs. [6] Love does not delight in evil but rejoices with the truth. [7] It always protects, always trusts, always hopes, always perseveres. [8] Love never fails. But where there are prophecies, they will cease; where there are tongues, they will be stilled; where there is

knowledge, it will pass away. [9] For we know in part and we prophesy in part, [10] but when perfection comes, the imperfect disappears. [11] When I was a child, I talked like a child, I thought like a child, I reasoned like a child. When I became a man, I put childish ways behind me. [12] Now we see but a poor reflection as in a mirror; then we shall see face to face. Now I know in part; then I shall know fully, even as I am fully known. [13] And now these three remain: faith, hope and love. But the greatest of these is love. (1 Corinthians 13).

Joy

The joy the Holy Spirit produces within the Christian is a spiritual joy. It is not like the joy of the world. The joy of the world is like the happiness of the world — it is here today if things are going well, but gone tomorrow if things fall apart. The joy the Holy Spirit gives us is rooted in the fact that we belong to God, and heaven is our destination. This stabilizes our joy so that we are not dependent on our circumstances, but rather we have joy in the bad times as well as the good. We do not alternate between moods of joy and gloom. This is a strengthening factor in our Christian walk.

[10] Nehemiah said, "Go and enjoy choice food and sweet drinks, and send some to those who have nothing prepared. This day is sacred to our Lord. Do not grieve, for the joy of the LORD is your strength." (Nehemiah 8:10).

The Bible speaks of joy in spite of suffering.

[6] You became imitators of us and of the Lord; in spite of severe suffering, you welcomed the message with the joy given by the Holy Spirit. (1 Thessalonians 1:6).

[10]...sorrowful, yet always rejoicing... (2 Corinthians 6:10).

Although joy is produced in us by the Holy Spirit, our conduct greatly affects the degree to which we benefit from it. If we are obedient we will experience it in abundance, but if we are disobedient we will lose it. Then we must repent and ask God to restore our joy, as David did.

> [12] Restore to me the joy of your salvation and grant me a willing spirit, to sustain me. (Psalm 51:12).

When things are going well for us we need to remember that our situation can change. It is not the circumstances of the moment that we are to base our joy on, but we should base it on the fact that Christ has saved us. Nothing can compare with salvation as a reason for joy. Christ points this out to the 72 disciples.

> [17] The seventy-two returned with joy and said, "Lord, even the demons submit to us in your name." [18] He replied, "I saw Satan fall like lightning from heaven. [19] I have given you authority to trample on snakes and scorpions and to overcome all the power of the enemy; nothing will harm you. [20] However, do not rejoice that the spirits submit to you, but rejoice that your names are written in heaven." (Luke 10:17-20).

Peter confirms the joy that believers have in their salvation.

> [8] Though you have not seen him, you love him; and even though you do not see him now, you believe in him and are filled with an inexpressible and glorious joy, [9] for you are receiving the goal of your faith, the salvation of your souls. (1 Peter 1:8-9).

Peace

Like joy, the peace given the Christian is different from that of the world.

> [27] Peace I leave with you; my peace I give you. I do not give to you as the world gives. Do not let your hearts be troubled and do not be afraid.
> (John 14:27).

When we come to Christ, we make peace with God.

> **1 Therefore, since we have been justified through faith, we have peace with God through our Lord Jesus Christ...** (Romans 5:1).

Having made peace with God we are to live in peace with fellow Christians and with all men, if possible.

> **13 Live in peace with each other.**
> (1 Thessalonians 5:13b).

> **14 Make every effort to live in peace with all men...**
> (Hebrews 12:14).

When we came to God through Christ, we not only ceased <u>hostility toward Him</u>, we also began <u>communion with Him</u>. We not only were made to be at peace with Him, but also were given peace by Him. However, if we are to continue to experience this peace and benefit from it, we must walk in obedience. We must be controlled by the Holy Spirit.

> **6...but the mind controlled by the Spirit is life and peace...** (Romans 8:6).

One of the benefits of this peace is that we no longer have to fret and worry about anything — health, finances, family, job, people, events, etc. We are not to be anxious over these things but are to put them before God in prayer. As we do this, we can have peace.

> **6 Do not be anxious about anything, but in everything, by prayer and petition, with thanksgiving, present your requests to God. 7 And the peace of God, which transcends all understanding, will guard your hearts and your minds in Christ Jesus.** (Philippians 4:6-7).

> **7 Cast all your anxiety on him because he cares for you.** (Peter 5:7).

These verses do not mean that we are not to have concern or exercise care; however, our faith in God's love for us, and in His sovereignty over all that touches us, will keep us from anxiety.

> [3] **You will keep in perfect peace him whose mind is steadfast, because he trusts in you.** (Isaiah 26:3).

We should not just remain at peace with others, but we are to encourage peace between others — between family members, friends, and fellow believers. We should look to God to use us as peacemakers, to help bring peace between man and man, and between God and man.

> [9] **Blessed are the peacemakers, for they will be called sons of God.** (Matthew 5:9).

> [18] **Peacemakers who sow in peace raise a harvest of righteousness.** (James 3:18).

Patience

Patience is next in the list of the fruit of the Spirit. This entails being patient under all circumstances, but particularly in the face of adversity and ill will. We are to be patient when provoked, and we are not to retaliate. As Christ is our perfect example of all that is good, He is our example for patience.

> [16] **But for that very reason I was shown mercy so that in me, the worst of sinners, Christ Jesus might display his unlimited patience as an example for those who would believe on him and receive eternal life.** (1 Timothy 1:16).

> [9] **The Lord is not slow in keeping his promise, as some understand slowness. He is patient with you, not wanting anyone to perish, but everyone to come to repentance.** (2 Peter 3:9).

We are admonished to be patient with everyone. Also, whether in affliction or under persecution, we are to be patient as we wait for the Lord's coming.

[7] Be patient, then, brothers, until the Lord's coming. See how the farmer waits for the land to yield its valuable crop and how patient he is for the autumn and spring rains. [8] You too, be patient and stand firm, because the Lord's coming is near. [9] Don't grumble against each other, brothers, or you will be judged. The Judge is standing at the door! [10] Brothers, as an example of patience in the face of suffering, take the prophets who spoke in the name of the Lord. [11] As you know, we consider blessed those who have persevered. You have heard of Job's perseverance and have seen what the Lord finally brought about. The Lord is full of compassion and mercy. (James 5:7-11).

[12] Be joyful in hope, patient in affliction, faithful in prayer. (Romans 12:12).

[14] And we urge you, brothers, warn those who are idle, encourage the timid, help the weak, be patient with everyone. (1 Thessalonians 5:14).

The Book of Proverbs contrasts patience to a quick temper.

[29] A patient man has great understanding, but a quick-tempered man displays folly.
(Proverbs 14:29).

[18] A hot-tempered man stirs up dissension, but a patient man calms a quarrel. (Proverbs 15:18).

[32] Better a patient man than a warrior, a man who controls his temper than one who takes a city.
(Proverbs 16:32).

We see that Abraham waited patiently for the promise of God.

[13] When God made his promise to Abraham, since there was no one greater for him to swear by, he swore by himself, [14] saying, "I will surely bless you and give you many descendants." [15] And so after waiting patiently, Abraham received what was promised. (Hebrews 6:13-15).

We, too, are to wait patiently on Christ. We are to cling to our hope of salvation, which is not the kind of hope the world knows, but a hope that rests in Christ — a hope that is sure.

> [17] For our light and momentary troubles are achieving for us an eternal glory that far outweighs them all. [18] So we fix our eyes not on what is seen, but on what is unseen. For what is seen is temporary, but what is unseen is eternal.
> (2 Corinthians 4:17-18).

> [25] But if we hope for what we do not yet have, we wait for it patiently. (Romans 8:25).

Kindness

Kindness suggests a mild or sweet temper, kind acts motivated by a regard for need, a politeness that goes beyond good manners, and manifests consideration for the fragile nature of human personality. God exercises kindness on earth, and His kindness is shown in His giving to and providing for mankind.

> [17] Yet he has not left himself without testimony: He has shown kindness by giving you rain from heaven and crops in their seasons; he provides you with plenty of food and fills your hearts with joy."
> (Acts 14:17).

We should tell others about God's kindness and praise Him for it. His kindness leads men toward repentance.

> [7] I will tell of the kindnesses of the LORD, the deeds for which he is to be praised, according to all the LORD has done for us— yes, the many good things he has done for the house of Israel, according to his compassion and many kindnesses. (Isaiah 63:7).

> [4] Or do you show contempt for the riches of his kindness, tolerance and patience, not realizing that God's kindness leads you toward repentance? (Romans 2:4).

We are examples of God's kindness, which is shown by His having saved us by grace.

> [6] And God raised us up with Christ and seated us with him in the heavenly realms in Christ Jesus, [7] in order that in the coming ages he might show the incomparable riches of his grace, expressed in his kindness to us in Christ Jesus. (Ephesians 2:6-7).

> [4] But when the kindness and love of God our Savior appeared, [5] he saved us... (Titus 3:4-5a).

With God as our example of kindness and the indwelling Spirit producing the fruit of kindness within us, we should seek to show God's kindness to others. Furthermore, God's Word tells us to be kind.

> [24] And the Lord's servant must not quarrel; instead, he must be kind to everyone, able to teach, not resentful. (2 Timothy 2:24).

> [32] Be kind and compassionate to one another, forgiving each other, just as in Christ God forgave you. (Ephesians 4:32).

> [15] Make sure that nobody pays back wrong for wrong, but always try to be kind to each other and to everyone else. (1 Thessalonians 5:15).

Goodness

Goodness is a perfect example of our total dependence on the Holy Spirit to do anything that is pleasing to God. There are many good men according to man's standard. There are none according to God's standard. God is the only one who is good.

> [17] As Jesus started on his way, a man ran up to him and fell on his knees before him. "Good teacher," he asked, "what must I do to inherit eternal life?" [18] "Why do you call me good?" Jesus answered. "No one is good—except God alone. (Mark 10:17-18).

> [2] The LORD looks down from heaven on the sons of men to see if there are any who understand, any who seek God. [3] All have turned aside, they have together become corrupt; there is no one who does good, not even one.
> (Psalm 14:2-3).

When you become a Christian, then the Spirit produces the fruit of goodness in you. God then considers you a good man, and He considers what you do in the power of the Spirit to be good work.

Goodness indicates being both morally and spiritually good, and will lead to <u>doing</u> good as a result of <u>being</u> good. As a good tree produces good fruit, so a good person does good deeds.

> [45] The good man brings good things out of the good stored up in his heart, and the evil man brings evil things out of the evil stored up in his heart. For out of the overflow of his heart his mouth speaks.
> (Luke 6:45).

As recipients of divine goodness and in obedience to divine will, we should strive to do good in both word and deed.

> [16] And do not forget to do good and to share with others, for with such sacrifices God is pleased.
> (Hebrews 13:16).
>
> [18] Command them to do good, to be rich in good deeds, and to be generous and willing to share.
> (1 Timothy 6:18).
>
> [7] In everything set them an example by doing what is good... (Titus 2:7).
>
> [10] Therefore, as we have opportunity, let us do good to all people, especially to those who belong to the family of believers. (Galatians 6:10).

It becomes obvious that if we are going to exemplify the fruit of goodness, we must concern ourselves with being helpful and seeking to benefit others by word and deed. We should even encourage other Christians to do good.

> **24 And let us consider how we may spur one another on toward love and good deeds.** (Hebrews 10:24).

We are to live such good lives and do such good deeds among unbelievers that our lives should give them nothing to be critical of. As a result, some of them may be won to Christ. It would only be out of ignorance or malice that they could accuse us of wrongdoing.

> **15 For it is God's will that by doing good you should silence the ignorant talk of foolish men.**
> (1 Peter 2:15).

> **12 Live such good lives among the pagans that, though they accuse you of doing wrong, they may see your good deeds and glorify God on the day he visits us.** (1 Peter 2:12).

We are even commanded to do good to our enemies. This becomes a real test of goodness in the Christian's life. Our response to this command shows whether or not we are being controlled by the Holy Spirit. God is kind to the ungrateful and wicked, and we are to be also.

> **35 But love your enemies, do good to them, and lend to them without expecting to get anything back. Then your reward will be great, and you will be sons of the Most High, because he is kind to the ungrateful and wicked.** (Luke 6:35).

We are not to repay evil for evil but are to repay evil with good. One very positive aspect to doing good is that in doing so we can overcome evil.

> **21 Do not be overcome by evil, but overcome evil with good.** (Romans 12:21).

This verse makes it clear that we are not only to resist being overcome by evil, but we are also to achieve victory over evil by doing good. This applies to all situations. In particular, it applies when someone has wronged us, and we are tempted to respond in a wrongful and unloving way. Instead, we are to love them and do good to them. Only as we allow the Holy Spirit to produce the fruit of goodness in us will we be able to respond in this manner.

Faithfulness

The fruit of faithfulness includes faithfulness to man as well as faithfulness to God. Faithfulness to God, though based on faith in God, is our faithfulness to serve God — our faithful obedience to God.

> [14] "Now fear the LORD and serve him with all faithfulness. (Joshua 24:14a).

Paul tells us that Tychicus was faithful in his service to the Lord.

> [21] Tychicus, the dear brother and faithful servant in the Lord, will tell you everything, so that you also may know how I am and what I am doing.
> (Ephesians 6:21).

God is our example of perfect faithfulness.

> [9] Know therefore that the LORD your God is God; he is the faithful God, keeping his covenant of love to a thousand generations of those who love him and keep his commands. (Deuteronomy 7:9).

> [2] For great is his love toward us, and the faithfulness of the LORD endures forever. Praise the LORD.
> (Psalm 117:2).

With God as our source and our example, we should seek to be faithful to our fellow man. A Christian who is faithful is someone who manifests fidelity, can be trusted to keep his word, and lives up to his promises. If we are faithful to God, it follows that we will be faithful to man. We will be faithful in the discharge of our duties, in taking care of our responsibilities, in fulfilling our commitments, in keeping our word and vows, in living up to our contracts, and in our relationships to others. As Christians, we should strive to be faithful and to remain faithful.

> [3] **Let love and faithfulness never leave you; bind them around your neck, write them on the tablet of your heart.** (Proverbs 3:3).

Gentleness

A gentle person does not give up his rights as a way of life, but may give them up on occasion. However, when retaining and defending his rights, he always does so with gentleness. When in a superior position, one who is gentle may yield to one beneath him. He may not press a legal right to its fullest in order to avoid causing the other party a problem. A gentle person is not violent, quarrelsome or harsh, but is friendly and considerate of others. The Bible tells us that God is gentle. Christ says for us to take His yoke because He is gentle.

> [11] **He tends his flock like a shepherd: He gathers the lambs in his arms and carries them close to his heart; he gently leads those that have young.** (Isaiah 40:11).

> [29] **Take my yoke upon you and learn from me, for I am gentle and humble in heart, and you will find rest for your souls.** (Matthew 11:29).

Paul appeals to the Corinthians in the gentleness of Christ.

> [1] **By the meekness and gentleness of Christ, I appeal to you...** (2 Corinthians 10:1a).

Scripture makes it clear that gentleness is expected of the Christian.

[1] **Brothers, if someone is caught in a sin, you who are spiritual should restore him gently.** (Galatians 6:1a).

[5] **Let your gentleness be evident to all. The Lord is near.** (Philippians 4:5).

Self-Control

Self-control is the last virtue listed as the fruit of the Spirit. Being listed last does not imply that it is any less a virtue or any less needed than the others. We have only to look at Scripture to see how prevalent the lack of self-control is among those who belong to the Lord. This evidence is backed up by our own personal experience and the observation of our fellow believers. Self-control is a virtue to be sought. Lack of self-control is a sin to be discarded. Like all the other virtues of the fruit of the Spirit, self-control can only be achieved in the power of the Holy Spirit. In one sense, it is the new self in us having control over the old self — our sinful nature.

There was a time when high walls were built around cities as protection against enemies. God says if we lack self-control we are like a city without walls, defenseless against the enemy. We are defenseless against temptation and against the enticement of Satan.

[28] **Like a city whose walls are broken down is a man who lacks self-control.** (Proverbs 25:28).

Self-control involves having control over our thoughts, desires, natural impulses, emotions, and actions. It encompasses not only resisting the desires of the flesh, but also restraint of any form of behavior such as anger and temper. It further includes moderation in those things that are neutral. A neutral thing out of control is no longer neutral, and it can be disruptive and even destructive to our Christian walk. This includes eating, watching TV, reading, etc. Paul and Peter both wrote of the need for self-controlled lives.

[6] So then, let us not be like others, who are asleep,
but let us be alert and self-controlled.
(1 Thessalonians 5:6).

[13] Therefore, prepare your minds for action; be self-
controlled... (1 Peter 1:13a).

Self-control calls for self-discipline. Solomon tells us
that one of the reasons for writing Proverbs was to help
people acquire a disciplined life.

[1] The proverbs of Solomon son of David, king of
Israel: [2] for attaining wisdom and discipline; for
understanding words of insight; [3] for acquiring a
disciplined and prudent life, doing what is right and
just and fair... (Proverbs 1:1-3).

Biblical self-control can be attained only if we are
operating in the power of the Holy Spirit. If we look to God to
make self-control a reality in our lives, He will bring it about.

[7] For God did not give us a spirit of timidity, but a
spirit of power, of love and of self-discipline.
(2 Timothy 1:7).

Paul says there is no law against the fruit of the Spirit.
These things are good, and there is no law against being
good or doing good. There is not only no law against them,
but the law cannot bring them into being. It cannot cause
them to be manifested. It is only by the work of the Holy
Spirit that they come about.

Gifts of The Spirit

Whereas the fruit of the Spirit has to do with our
character, the gifts of the Spirit have bearing on our works.
These gifts are given to us by God and are to be used in the
work of God. All Christians have at least one gift, and some
Christians have more than one. They should be exercised at
the direction of the Holy Spirit and in His strength.

[10] Each one should use whatever gift he has received to serve others, faithfully administering God's grace in its various forms. [11] If anyone speaks, he should do it as one speaking the very words of God. If anyone serves, he should do it with the strength God provides, so that in all things God may be praised through Jesus Christ. To him be the glory and the power for ever and ever. Amen.
(1 Peter 4:10-11).

The Holy Spirit has different work for each of us to do, and He gives His gifts and grace to us as needed to accomplish His purpose.

[4] There are different kinds of gifts, but the same Spirit. [5] There are different kinds of service, but the same Lord. [6] There are different kinds of working, but the same God works all of them in all men. [7] Now to each one the manifestation of the Spirit is given for the common good. [8] To one there is given through the Spirit the message of wisdom, to another the message of knowledge by means of the same Spirit, [9] to another faith by the same Spirit, to another gifts of healing by that one Spirit, [10] to another miraculous powers, to another prophecy, to another distinguishing between spirits, to another speaking in different kinds of tongues, and to still another the interpretation of tongues. [11] All these are the work of one and the same Spirit, and he gives them to each one, just as he determines.
(1 Corinthians 12:4-11).

[27] Now you are the body of Christ, and each one of you is a part of it. [28] And in the church God has appointed first of all apostles, second prophets, third teachers, then workers of miracles, also those having gifts of healing, those able to help others, those with gifts of administration, and those speaking in different kinds of tongues. [29] Are all apostles? Are all prophets? Are all teachers? Do all work miracles? [30] Do all have gifts of healing? Do all speak in tongues? Do all interpret? [31] But eagerly desire the greater gifts. (1 Corinthians 12:27-31).

[3] **For by the grace given me I say to every one of you: Do not think of yourself more highly than you ought, but rather think of yourself with sober judgment, in accordance with the measure of faith God has given you.** [4] **Just as each of us has one body with many members, and these members do not all have the same function,** [5] **so in Christ we who are many form one body, and each member belongs to all the others.** [6] **We have different gifts, according to the grace given us. If a man's gift is prophesying, let him use it in proportion to his faith.** [7] **If it is serving, let him serve; if it is teaching, let him teach;** [8] **if it is encouraging, let him encourage; if it is contributing to the needs of others, let him give generously; if it is leadership, let him govern diligently; if it is showing mercy, let him do it cheerfully.** (Romans 12:3-8).

Paul brings out a point in Romans 12:3 that we all should heed. Whatever our gift or gifts are, we are not to think more highly of ourselves than is warranted. We are not to think, much less claim, that we have gifts and abilities that we do not possess. On the other hand, we should not go too far in the other direction and deny gifts and abilities that the Holy Spirit has given us. Either way is wrong. Our task is to take a realistic look at what our gifts are and, by His grace, use them as He directs. If we do not use our gifts the work and edification of the church will suffer. If we do not know what our gift or gifts are but we want to use them, then we need to stay controlled by the Holy Spirit. He knows what they are, and He will see that we use them.

It appears that there are 17 to 20 gifts of the Spirit listed in the Bible, depending on who is doing the counting. However, we do not know if there are gifts that are not listed. We should not close our minds to the fact that the Holy Spirit may give us a new task five years from now, and a new gift by which to accomplish it. Let us not forget that He determines what will be done, and He gives the gifts at His own pleasure.

Blasphemy Against The Holy Spirit

Blasphemy against the Holy Spirit is often referred to as the unpardonable sin. Gospel references to it are Matthew 12:31-32, Mark 3:28-29, and Luke 12:10. These verses do not tell us exactly what blasphemy against the Holy Spirit is. As a result, expositors have differing opinions about it. Let us look at how this is stated in Matthew.

> [22] Then they brought him a demon-possessed man who was blind and mute, and Jesus healed him, so that he could both talk and see. [23] All the people were astonished and said, "Could this be the Son of David?" [24] But when the Pharisees heard this, they said, "It is only by Beelzebub, the prince of demons, that this fellow drives out demons." [25] Jesus knew their thoughts and said to them, "Every kingdom divided against itself will be ruined, and every city or household divided against itself will not stand. [26] If Satan drives out Satan, he is divided against himself. How then can his kingdom stand? [27] And if I drive out demons by Beelzebub, by whom do your people drive them out? So then, they will be your judges. [28] But if I drive out demons by the Spirit of God, then the kingdom of God has come upon you. [29] "Or again, how can anyone enter a strong man's house and carry off his possessions unless he first ties up the strong man? Then he can rob his house. [30] "He who is not with me is against me, and he who does not gather with me scatters. [31] And so I tell you, every sin and blasphemy will be forgiven men, but the blasphemy against the Spirit will not be forgiven. [32] Anyone who speaks a word against the Son of Man will be forgiven, but anyone who speaks against the Holy Spirit will not be forgiven, either in this age or in the age to come. (Matthew 12:22-32).

Some expositors say that the blasphemy is the failure to believe the message of the Holy Spirit about Christ. Others put it stronger and say it is a willful and defiant disbelief of the Holy Spirit's message. In both of these cases those who do not believe in Christ are condemned to hell. That is a stated fact throughout Scripture. However, blasphemy against the Spirit seems to be something more specific. Some say it is calling good bad and bad good. I feel that this is a little broad and somewhat vague. Others say it is attributing the work of Christ, in calling out the demons, to Satan instead of to the Holy Spirit. I believe this is more in line with what is said, but it is possibly too specific.

It is easier for me to accept the exposition of those who say it is attributing any of the miraculous works of Christ to Satan instead of to the Holy Spirit. However, regardless of what blasphemy against the Spirit is, one thing is certain: A child of God will not commit it. Those who commit it are eternally lost; however, a child of God is eternally saved. If we are saved it is because we are of the Elect. God chose to save us; therefore, those whom God has chosen to save will be saved. Otherwise, God is limited in what He can do. If God is limited, then He is not God. No, if we are Christians we do not have to worry about committing the unpardonable sin. By God's grace, this is another blessing we enjoy. We are saved, and we will remain saved — we cannot be lost. God is the one who saves us, and He is the one who will keep us saved. It is true that we must endure to the end, but it is equally true that God's Holy Spirit will see that we do.

> [3] **Praise be to the God and Father of our Lord Jesus Christ! In his great mercy he has given us new birth into a living hope through the resurrection of Jesus Christ from the dead,** [4] **and into an inheritance that can never perish, spoil or fade—kept in heaven for you,** [5] **who through faith are shielded by God's power until the coming of the salvation that is ready to be revealed in the last time.** (1 Peter 1:3-5).

> [24] **To him who is able to keep you from falling and to present you before his glorious presence without fault and with great joy**... (Jude 24).

> [8] He will keep you strong to the end, so that you will be blameless on the day of our Lord Jesus Christ. [9] God, who has called you into fellowship with his Son Jesus Christ our Lord, is faithful.
> (1 Corinthians 1:8-9).

Sanctification And The Holy Spirit

From a perspective of both doctrine and experience, a number of Christians know much about salvation, but know little about sanctification. Sanctification is the ongoing work of the Holy Spirit in the lives of believers.

> [23] May God himself, the God of peace, sanctify you through and through. May your whole spirit, soul and body be kept blameless at the coming of our Lord Jesus Christ. (1 Thessalonians 5:23).

How successful our sanctification is depends on our willingness to submit to the control of the Holy Spirit. As our thoughts, words, and deeds reflect what is in our hearts, our lives should not only show that we have been justified before God, but that we are also being sanctified by God.

> [33] "Make a tree good and its fruit will be good, or make a tree bad and its fruit will be bad, for a tree is recognized by its fruit. (Matthew 12:33).

Fruit cannot make the tree good or bad. It can only indicate that it is good or bad. The tree comes first and the type of tree will determine the type of fruit. A lack of fruit indicates a useless tree — one that is taking up space without producing fruit.

> [6] Then he told this parable: "A man had a fig tree, planted in his vineyard, and he went to look for fruit on it, but did not find any. [7] So he said to the man who took care of the vineyard, 'For three years now I've been coming to look for fruit on this fig tree and haven't found any. Cut it down! Why should it use

> up the soil?' [8] "'Sir,' the man replied, 'leave it alone
> for one more year, and I'll dig around it and fertilize
> it. [9] If it bears fruit next year, fine! If not, then cut it
> down.'" (Luke 13:6-9).

Because the tree comes before the fruit, we should
concern ourselves not as much with our "doing" as with our
"being." If the tree is good, it will not only bear fruit, it will
bear good fruit. All Christians are expected to bear good
fruit. Moreover, in the process of sanctification, the Holy
Spirit is pruning us to make us even more fruitful.

> [1] "I am the true vine, and my Father is the gardener. [2]
> He cuts off every branch in me that bears no fruit,
> while every branch that does bear fruit he prunes so
> that it will be even more fruitful. (John 15:1-2).

Because we live in an achievement oriented society
some Christians can be confused as to just what is suppose
to take place in their sanctification. They think of it as a
process of doing more and more good deeds when it
actually is a process of becoming more and more like Christ.
The Christian is predestined to be conformed to the likeness
of Christ, and the Holy Spirit works in our sanctification to
make us more and more like Christ.

> [29] For those God foreknew he also predestined to be
> conformed to the likeness of his Son, that he might
> be the firstborn among many brothers.
> (Romans 8:29).

If we are to grow more like Christ we must know more about
Christ. We are told to grow in the knowledge of Christ.

> [18] But grow in the grace and knowledge of our Lord
> and Savior Jesus Christ. (2 Peter 3:18a).

We must learn in order to become and as we become we
are then ready to do. We must "know" the Bible before we
can teach the Bible. We must learn what to do and how to do
before we set out to do. And there is only one way this can
be done — through the Holy Spirit. He is our teacher.

> [26] But the Counselor, the Holy Spirit, whom the
> Father will send in my name, will teach you all things
> and will remind you of everything I have said to you.
> (John 14:26).

In our sanctification we should constantly be looking to the Holy Spirit to teach us and to grow us spiritually. When we come to doctrines in the Bible that are hard to understand or that are hard to accept, we should study the doctrines while asking the Spirit to teach us the truth.

An example of something that the Bible teaches that many Christians have a problem with is creation. They have been taught evolution, which is contrary to creation. Evolution is taught in public schools, in TV documentaries, in newspaper and magazine articles, etc. Even though evolution is only a theory and has not been proven to be true, it is taught as fact. Many Christians find themselves in a dilemma — whether to believe the Bible or believe all the scientists who push evolution. So they often try to reconcile the Bible with evolution. It can't be done.

For anyone who has a problem believing the Biblical account of creation, I suggest you read the account in the Book of Genesis and pay close attention to the details. Notice that God says all the creatures were created according to their kind. They did not evolve from another kind.

> [24] And God said, "Let the land produce living
> creatures according to their kinds: livestock,
> creatures that move along the ground, and wild
> animals, each according to its kind." And it was so.
> [25] God made the wild animals according to their
> kinds, the livestock according to their kinds, and all
> the creatures that move along the ground according
> to their kinds. And God saw that it was good.
> (Genesis 1:24-25).

When first created, man did not eat animals and the animals did not eat each other. They all ate plants.

> [29] Then God said, "I give you every seed-bearing
> plant on the face of the whole earth and every tree

> that has fruit with seed in it. They will be yours for food. [30] And to all the beasts of the earth and all the birds of the air and all the creatures that move on the ground—everything that has the breath of life in it—I give every green plant for food." And it was so. (Genesis 1:29-30).

It was only after "The Fall" of man (when Adam sinned) that man ate animals and animals ate each other.

> [12] Therefore, just as sin entered the world through one man, and death through sin, and in this way death came to all men, because all sinned... (Romans 5:12).

> [1] Then God blessed Noah and his sons, saying to them, "Be fruitful and increase in number and fill the earth. [2] The fear and dread of you will fall upon all the beasts of the earth and all the birds of the air, upon every creature that moves along the ground, and upon all the fish of the sea; they are given into your hands. [3] Everything that lives and moves will be food for you. Just as I gave you the green plants, I now give you everything. (Genesis 9:1-3).

I suggest you consider one other thing. Think of how few people there are that are truly Christians compared to the total population. It will be a small number. Then consider most groups of people such as policemen, doctors, firemen, construction workers, teachers, and factory workers. Within each group there will be a small number that are truly Christians just as there is in the total population. This also will hold true for scientists. Because there is such a large number of scientists who believe in evolution, their voices are heard over those people who speak out for creation. Therefore, evolution is being presented in such a manner that, if you believe it, you are intelligent. If you don't believe it, you are either not very smart or you are a religious fanatic. The pure evolutionist doesn't believe in an eternal God, he believes in eternal matter. The theistic evolutionist believes that God created everything through evolution. Being swayed by science he tries to make the Bible support science. He is not far removed from those who believe in intelligent design. They try to make the Bible <u>appealing</u> to science. Theistic evolution and intelligent design both have creation taking place over millions of years. This means that death and suffering were in the world before man sinned. But the Bible tells us that death only came into the world when man (Adam) sinned.

> [12] **Therefore, just as sin entered the world through one man, and death through sin, and in this way death came to all men, because all sinned...** (Romans 5:12).

God says He created everything in six days, not over millions of years. (See Chapter 1 of Genesis).

For those who do believe in creation, but have doubts from time to time, let me say, don't be discouraged — God is on our side. He has scientists who are Christians, and they help us understand the errors in the information being put out by the evolutionists. Two excellent organizations of these scientists are "Answers in Genesis" located in Hebron, Kentucky (www.AnswersInGenesis.org) and the "Institute for Creation Research" located in El Cajon, California (www.icr.org). Let us look to the Holy Spirit to teach us the truth about all doctrines, including those that are controversial like creation, sovereignty, predestination, election, etc.

Although sanctification is the work of the Holy Spirit, it is our responsibility to desire it, pray for it, and strive after it. We are called to be receptive to the work of the Holy Spirit; moreover, we are to be actively responsive to it. Our action is in response to the prompting of the Holy Spirit. Equally important, our action is to be at His direction and in His power. In sanctification, God is totally active, and we are to be totally active. He is continually working in us to will and to do, and we are to continually will and do that which He works in us. As we do this we are working <u>out</u> our salvation, not working <u>for</u> it.

> **[12] Therefore, my dear friends, as you have always obeyed—not only in my presence, but now much more in my absence—continue to work out your salvation with fear and trembling...** (Philippians 2:12).

The Christian life begins at the time of our salvation and is lived through the process of sanctification. The Holy Spirit does more than bring us to salvation — He gives us a desire to serve God. He causes us to seek to know God's will and then to seek to do it. If we do not want to do God's will, we are not under the control of the Holy Spirit — we may not even have the Spirit.

How To Be Controlled By The Spirit

Let us look closely at what we must do to live a Spirit-controlled life. First, we must desire the Holy Spirit to control our lives. It will mean doing God's will — not our will. It will mean denying self, doing things God's way — not our way — and doing things in God's strength instead of in the flesh. It will mean taking a totally different view of those so-called little sins that many Christians consider harmless. God says for us to be holy for He is holy, and a holy God cannot tolerate <u>any</u> sin.

> **[16] for it is written: "Be holy, because I am holy."**
> (1 Peter 1:16).

Second, it will mean exerting our will. We must will to do God's will. We must not only want the Holy Spirit to control us, but we must actively will to have the Holy Spirit in control. We must confess our sins and ask God to control us by His Holy Spirit. We do this through faith, believing what God's Word says.

By faith we believe our sins are forgiven.

> **[9] If we confess our sins, he is faithful and just and will forgive us our sins and purify us from all unrighteousness.** (1 John 1:9).

By faith we believe God wants us to be controlled by the Holy Spirit.

> [18] Do not get drunk on wine, which leads to debauchery. Instead, be filled with the Spirit. (Ephesians 5:18).

By faith we believe God will control us through His Holy Spirit if we ask Him.

> [14] This is the confidence we have in approaching God: that if we ask anything according to his will, he hears us. [15] And if we know that he hears us— whatever we ask—we know that we have what we asked of him. (1 John 5:14-15).

We act in faith to please God and to receive the promise of being controlled by the Holy Spirit.

> [6] And without faith it is impossible to please God, because anyone who comes to him must believe that he exists and that he rewards those who earnestly seek him. (Hebrews 11:6).

> [6] But when he asks, he must believe and not doubt, because he who doubts is like a wave of the sea, blown and tossed by the wind. [7] That man should not think he will receive anything from the Lord; [8] he is a double-minded man, unstable in all he does. (James 1:6-8).

We know it is His will that we be controlled. If, in obedience to His will, we ask in faith to be controlled, then what will happen? We will be controlled — the Holy Spirit will control us. God promises this to be the result. When we ask according to His will, He will give us what we ask.

You may ask: "Once I am controlled, then what?" My answer is, do your best to see that the Holy Spirit stays in control of your life. Then He will guide and direct you to do that which pleases Him.

Will this be the way it is from now on? No, not if you are like me and all the other Christians I have known. The teaching of the Bible is that from time to time our sinful nature will exert itself, and we will take over the control of our lives from the Holy Spirit.

> [16] **So I say, live by the Spirit, and you will not gratify the desires of the sinful nature.** [17] **For the sinful nature desires what is contrary to the Spirit, and the Spirit what is contrary to the sinful nature. They are in conflict with each other, so that you do not do what you want.** (Galatians 5:16-17).

Our taking over control of our lives will grieve the Holy Spirit and break the fellowship we were enjoying with God. We always have our relationship as a child of God, but our fellowship is dependent on our obedience to God. Unless the Holy Spirit is controlling us, we are being disobedient. We are failing to obey a command from God. We are sinning and as a result, our fellowship with God is broken. However, we are not to be discouraged, but are to turn to God, confess that we have taken over control, and once again ask His Holy Spirit to control our lives. We can then know that the Holy Spirit is back in control, and that we have fellowship with God. As long as He is in control, we will not sin.

Every time we realize that we have resumed control of our lives (and sometimes we resume control in very subtle ways), we need to go through the process of actively confessing our sins and asking God to control our lives by His Holy Spirit. As we make a practice of doing this, we will find that we grow spiritually and do not have to go through the process as often as we once did. However, if at first we need to do it every 30 minutes, we should do so. It can help us to remember to do this if we turn a ring or our watch around. A good Bible teacher I sat under suggested putting something in our pocket as a reminder. The important thing is to will to do it, and make the commitment to do it. Start now — before you lay this book down.

Just as unbelievers can pray in faith to be saved, believers can pray in faith to be controlled by the Holy Spirit.

You may want to pray the following prayer or something similar, as you feel led:

Dear God, I confess I have sinned, and I ask you to please forgive my sins and to control me by your Holy Spirit. I ask this in Jesus' name. Amen.

We should pray like this each time we realize that we have sinned, and whenever we realize that we are in control of our lives, or when we have doubts as to who is in control. If we have failed for a period of time to check ourselves to see who is in control we may have doubts about who is. However, when we pray and ask God to take control, we should never doubt, but always trust that He will do what He has promised. Keep in mind that we are not controlled by the Holy Spirit because we feel controlled, nor are we not controlled because we do not feel controlled. It is not a matter of how we feel. It is a matter of what God has willed and what God has promised to do when we respond in obedience to His will. It will happen when we ask in faith according to His will.

Evidence That We Are Controlled

If being controlled by the Holy Spirit does not depend on how we feel (it does not depend on feelings anymore than our salvation depends on our "feeling saved"), then we may wonder if there are any indications that we are really being controlled by the Holy Spirit. Yes, there are. When the trend of our lives is that of being controlled by the Spirit, we begin to actually see our lives changing more than we did before. Changes in our values, our desires, and our attitudes are greater and more rapid. There is a greater appreciation for what the Bible calls good, and a greater dislike of what the Bible calls sin. We are conscious of sinning less, and we begin to develop intolerance for sin in our lives. There is a greater desire to read and study God's Word, and a real concern to know and to do God's will.

As we practice walking in the Spirit, we will have a better understanding of God, His written Word, and ourselves. We see God changing us, and this glorifies Him because we know He is doing it. We see Him working through us, using us as instruments or mere tools to accomplish His work in others. We begin to receive a much greater degree of pleasure when God uses us. We derive great pleasure from watching Him work. We find that seeing God glorified becomes more than talk; it actually becomes the goal of our life.

Walking in the Spirit

[25] Since we live by the Spirit, let us keep in step with the Spirit. (Galatians 5:25).

A rough idea of walking in the Spirit would be the following illustration that I once heard: Imagine you are painting a picture, and you know absolutely nothing about art. As a result, you are making somewhat of a mess of the painting. But, along comes a master artist who reaches over your shoulder and takes your wrist. You still hold the brush, but the artist tells you to let your arm be limber. Then he begins to move your arm so that a beautiful picture is being formed. If you decide you want to help or you think the artist is not doing it right and you stiffen your arm and make some strokes, you begin to make a mess of the painting again. Only as you let your arm remain limber and allow the artist to move it, is the picture painted correctly. Only then does it become the picture it is possible for it to be.

This is true of our walk with God. Only as we keep our wills limber and let God direct our thoughts, words, and actions will our lives be lived correctly. Only then will they become what it is possible for them to be.

Live Under The Control Of The Holy Spirit

As we come to the close of our discussion of the Holy Spirit, it is my hope that each of us is well aware of our need to live continually under His control. If we understand and believe that the Holy Spirit regenerates us and enables us to trust Christ, then it will be easier for us to recognize our need of Him to live the Christian life. On the other hand, if we do not believe that it was the work of the Holy Spirit, but believe we trusted Christ on our own, then it may be more difficult for us to see the need for Him now. If the Holy Spirit did not enable us to trust Christ, then we did it in our own strength. Why then could we not live the Christian life in our own strength? Of course, that type of thinking is totally wrong — it is not Scriptural — it robs God of His glory. If we are to obey God it can only be done under the control of the Holy Spirit. It is our only hope of pleasing God and our only hope of overcoming sin. The alternative to being under the control of the Spirit is to be under the control of our sinful nature. Because nothing but evil comes from the sinful nature and nothing but good comes from the Holy Spirit, it becomes readily apparent why being controlled by the Spirit is so vital. We must look to the Holy Spirit to guide us in how we spend our time, where we spend it, and with whom we spend it.

Bill Bright, the Founder of Campus Crusade For Christ, said that the most important message he had for the Christian was that of explaining the need for, and the how to, of being filled (controlled by) with the Holy Spirit.

D. M. Lloyd-Jones, in his book Life In The Spirit says the following:

There is only one way to live the truly Christian life; it is to be `filled with the Spirit`. It is a waste of breath to appeal to people to be better, it is a waste of breath to appeal to people in terms of Remembrance Sunday, the horrors of war, and so forth. They may become a little emotional, and be better for the rest of the day, perhaps it will cover even *the next day. But it will soon be gone like the morning dew, just as our New Year's resolutions are forgotten every year with such constant regularity. Man cannot do it. Man needs a new nature. He needs to be changed; and the Spirit of God alone can do that. Man needs to be `filled with the Spirit`. Then he will be able to do these things, and not until then.*

The Holy Spirit is sent to regenerate men, to give them a new nature, a new mind, a new outlook, a new everything. There is no hope apart from that. He is, likewise, sent in order to promote our sanctification — `Be filled with the Spirit`. It is only those who are controlled by the Holy Spirit of God who can live in peace with one another. This is the solution to the marriage problem, to the home problem, to the industrial problem. Once men are governed and filled by the Spirit, they understand, they see the evil that is in them, they curb and control themselves, they `grow in grace, and in the knowledge of the Lord`, amity and concord become a possibility. But only as they are `filled with the Spirit`. Without the Spirit it is impossible. So the Holy Spirit is meant and sent to promote our sanctification, and to control us, to enable us to live the life that God would have us live.

The Spirit leads us, not as one going before us to show us the way, but as one holding on to us and guiding us along. He is not showing us how to get where we want to go but is taking us where He chooses. We are like a blind man; we cannot see where we are to go or how to get there. The Spirit picks our destination and then leads us by the hand. We can think of ourselves as children holding our heavenly Father's hand. As long as we are holding His hand, the Holy Spirit is in control of our lives, and we will not stumble. However, when we let go of His hand by taking over control of our lives, we will stumble, and we must reach up to grab His hand again. In our own strength and wisdom, we are unable to live the Christian life. This can only be accomplished as we live under the control of the Holy Spirit.

[6] **'Not by might nor by power, but by my Spirit,' says the LORD Almighty.** (Zechariah 4:6b).

[13] **Now all has been heard; here is the conclusion of the matter: Fear God and keep his commandments, for this is the whole duty of man.** (Ecclesiastes 12:13).

A GRATEFUL HEART

I am grateful to You dear God for what you have done for me, in me, and through me. How blessed I am.

I am grateful to you dear Heavenly Father that you chose this undeserving sinner to be saved.

I am grateful to you dear Jesus Christ that you came, suffered, and died to pay the penalty for my sins.

I am grateful to you dear Holy Spirit that you made me spiritually alive and that you indwell me, teach me, enable me, and empower me in my walk with God.

I am grateful to you dear Lord for leading me and enabling me by Your Holy Spirit to write this, my fourth book, as well as the first three. I pray that You will use all four of these books to save some and to work spiritual maturity in some — thereby bringing honor and glory to Yourself. It is my hope that You will continue to do this by moving these books through many hands over the next 100 years.

Dear Lord, You saved me when I was 41 and I am now 81. However, I pray that You will continue to enable me to pass out these books to those You intend to have them. I pray Dear Heavenly Father as the Psalmist did, to be used by You in my old age.

[18] Even when I am old and gray, do not forsake me, O God, till I declare your power to the next generation, your might to all who are to come. (Psalm 71:18).

The Author's Testimony

Before I became a Christian, I thought I was one. I had always believed there was a God and that Jesus was the Son of God. I lived in a Christian country, was a member of a church, and I accepted the fact that Jesus died for the sins of the world. I felt this made me a Christian. I believed I would go to heaven when I died, although I had no real basis for believing it. I believed that some people would go to hell, but, like most everyone, I thought it would always happen to the other fellow. I knew I was a sinner who did some wrong things. However, I knew that I tried to be a good citizen, husband, and father. I felt the good I did out weighed the bad. I thought that in comparing my good and bad deeds, I was keeping the scales tipped in my favor. I envisioned that when this world is brought to an end, if all the people who had ever lived stood in a long line before the gates of heaven and God made a cut-off, the people on one side going to heaven and those on the other side going to hell, I would be on the side that got into heaven. I did not expect to be at the front of the line, but I did expect to make the cut-off.

There came a time in my life when I realized how fortunate I was. I had a nice home, a good marriage, two fine children (too young to get into real trouble), and good health. My wife Peg and I both felt blessed. Sometimes we would sit in our kitchen drinking coffee and wonder what life was all about. We wondered if enjoying life, as we were, and then one day dying with the uncertain hope of going to heaven was all there was to life. We became restless as we continued to wonder about the purpose of life.

My job required some travel, and while traveling I would often listen to preachers on the car radio. Looking back, I feel sure some were good and some were not, but I did not know the difference. However, I heard and understood enough to make me question if I was truly a Christian. I found myself praying as I drove, asking God to please make my family and me Christians.

Peg started taking our children to Sunday school. She felt it would be good for them, and I certainly agreed. She would attend an adult class while the children were in their classes. She suggested that I might want to join them, and I did. With time Peg and I became very religious – attending Sunday school and church on a regular basis. Peg became active in the women's work, and I became an officer of the church. We even helped to start a mission church. We were religious but not saved. We still carried the guilt of sin and were still under the penalty of sin. We were religiously active, but spiritually dead. If we had died while in that condition, we would have gone straight to hell.

My younger sister Mitzi told us about a lady, Elizabeth Newbold, who was a Bible teacher. It seemed that Elizabeth said the Bible taught that to be a Christian, a person had to have a personal relationship with Jesus Christ. Mitzi said that she now had this relationship. Peg and I did not understand what she meant by a "personal relationship" with Christ, but we decided to find out.

One night I called Elizabeth. I told her that I was Mitzi's brother, and that Peg and I would like to talk with her. She said that she had to go to Huntsville the next day to teach a Bible class, but would come to our house that night when she got back. Wanting to be a gentleman and do the right thing, I told her we would come to her house. However, she insisted on coming to ours. The next night we got a phone call about 9:30. Elizabeth had just gotten back from Huntsville, and it would be 10:30 before she could get to our house. She wanted to know if that was too late for us. The time was fine with us, but I felt it was too late for her. However, again she insisted. The fact that she was so eager and willing to do this for strangers made us even more desirous of hearing what she had to say.

We had made a list of questions to ask Elizabeth, and she obligingly answered them. However, she kept returning the conversation to the Gospel. She made us aware that we were counting on living lives good enough to deserve heaven. In other words, we were attempting to earn the right to go there when we died. She showed us where the Bible says that no one is saved by good deeds. We found that we could not tip the scales in our favor by doing good — our good deeds could not erase the sin on our record.

Elizabeth explained that God would not allow sin into heaven. She then pointed out that if we have committed just one sin, it is the same as breaking all of God's Law. We realized that no matter how hard we tried, we could not live the life God requires — life without any sin. And even if that were now possible, we were already condemned by our past sin. It became clear that we were lost sinners, without hope and headed to hell.

Elizabeth had given us the bad news. Next, she gave us the good news. She told us that Christ had died for us. He had already paid for every sin we had ever committed in the past, and every one we would ever commit in the future. Christ had lived a sinless life, suffered and died for our sins, was resurrected, and had ascended to heaven. He offered us the free gift of salvation. We could go to heaven because of what Christ did for us, not because of anything we do. He did it all. We could contribute nothing. Our sin debt was paid in full; all we needed to do was accept the gift.

Elizabeth pointed out that because it seems so simple, many people have trouble believing it. She explained that we should acknowledge that we were sinners, repent, ask Jesus Christ to forgive us and to come into our hearts and lives as our Savior and Lord. She explained that this involved more than an intellectual assent of fact about Jesus. It is a personal thing. A person must not only believe about Jesus, but must personally commit his life to Him, trusting and relying on Him to save him.

She then asked us if we would like to receive Christ as Savior and Lord. We were both only too glad to be able to do so, and about one o'clock in the morning, we knelt in our living room and asked Christ to save us. He did, and our lives were changed.

This was in the early part of 1966. We no longer had reason to wonder what life was all about. We soon learned we were to live and serve God in whatever way pleased Him. We were now Christians and the purpose of the Christian life was to glorify God.

Before I became a Christian, there were things that I knew were wrong to do, but I did them anyway. After Christ saved me, I tried to stop doing those things. One of the first things I stopped was cursing. In time I found there were things that were sinful that I had never thought of before as being sinful. Like all Christians, I sinned even though I did not want to or intend to. And like all Christians, I still sin today. We will not reach perfection and be without sin until we get to heaven. However, as time passes, I sin less and less as I learn, by God's grace, to walk more consistently in the control and power of His Holy Spirit.

When I do sin, I know I can turn to God and, in the name of His precious Son Jesus Christ, ask Him to forgive me — and He does. Having been forgiven so much by God, I want to be forgiving of others. I would hope that anyone I have wronged, intentionally of unintentionally, would forgive me too. However, all wrongdoing is actually sin against God, and it is His forgiveness that we must have. I am fully confident that I have God's forgiveness based on the fact that Christ paid the penalty for my sins. I received the benefit of His payment when I accepted Him as my Savior and Lord. I have confidence that I will go to heaven when I die, not because I deserve to, but because God has promised salvation to all who put their trust in His Son. Knowing that I do not deserve heaven makes me very grateful to God for His love and mercy in saving me.

I think it is normal for Christians, having experienced the joy of salvation, to want to tell others how they might come to know Christ personally. We want our families, friends, and strangers to hear the Good News about salvation. That is one reason this book and my first three books were written. It is my hope that, through these books, many who do not know Christ will come to a saving knowledge of Him.

Ed McDavid III

READER'S RESPONSE

Dear Reader,

I hope God has used this book in your life. While writing it, I prayed that He would use it to save souls and to work spiritual maturity in those who are already saved. I would be most grateful for any confirmation that this is being done. I give away copies of this book through my ministry of "Search the Scriptures." If the book is having a meaningful impact on people's lives, I want to continue to give away copies as the Lord leads and provides.

If, as a result of reading this book, you have received Jesus Christ as your Lord and Savior, trusting Him to forgive your sins and save you, please let me know.

If you were saved before reading this book, but now feel you have a better understanding of how dependent you are on the Holy Spirit to live the Christian life, and are committed to making an effort to have Him control you day by day, moment by moment, please let me know.

If this book has been meaningful or helpful to you in some other way, please let me know. Write me at the address below or, if you prefer, check any of the circles shown on this page and cut it out and mail it to me. Thank you.

As a result of reading this book:

O I received Christ as my Savior and Lord.
O I am trying to let the Holy Spirit control my life.
O Other remarks or questions:

_____
_____
_____
_____

Mail to: Ed McDavid
         Search the Scriptures
         P. O. Box 131447
         Birmingham, AL 35213

ROMANS CHAPTER 8

[1] Therefore, there is now no condemnation for those who are in Christ Jesus, [2] because through Christ Jesus the law of the Spirit of life set me free from the law of sin and death. [3] For what the law was powerless to do in that it was weakened by the sinful nature, God did by sending his own Son in the likeness of sinful man to be a sin offering. And so he condemned sin in sinful man, [4] in order that the righteous requirements of the law might be fully met in us, who do not live according to the sinful nature but according to the Spirit. [5] Those who live according to the sinful nature have their minds set on what that nature desires; but those who live in accordance with the Spirit have their minds set on what the Spirit desires. [6] The mind of sinful man is death, but the mind controlled by the Spirit is life and peace; [7] the sinful mind is hostile to God. It does not submit to God's law, nor can it do so. [8] Those controlled by the sinful nature cannot please God. [9] You, however, are controlled not by the sinful nature but by the Spirit, if the Spirit of God lives in you. And if anyone does not have the Spirit of Christ, he does not belong to Christ. [10] But if Christ is in you, your body is dead because of sin, yet your spirit is alive because of righteousness. [11] And if the Spirit of him who raised Jesus from the dead is living in you, he who raised Christ from the dead will also give life to your mortal bodies through his Spirit, who lives in you. [12] Therefore, brothers, we have an obligation—but it is not to the sinful nature, to live according to it. [13] For if you live according to the sinful nature, you will die; but if by the Spirit you put to death the misdeeds of the body, you will live, [14] because those who are led by the Spirit of God are sons of God. [15] For you did not receive a spirit that makes you a slave again to fear, but you received the Spirit of sonship. And by him we cry, *"Abba,* Father." [16] The Spirit himself testifies with our spirit that we are God's children. [17] Now if we are children, then we are heirs—heirs of God and co-heirs with Christ, if indeed we share in his sufferings in order that we may also share in his glory. [18] I consider that our present sufferings are not worth comparing with the glory that will be revealed in us. [19] The creation waits in eager expectation for the sons of God to be revealed. [20] For the creation was subjected to frustration, not by its own

choice, but by the will of the one who subjected it, in hope [21] that the creation itself will be liberated from its bondage to decay and brought into the glorious freedom of the children of God. [22] We know that the whole creation has been groaning as in the pains of childbirth right up to the present time. [23] Not only so, but we ourselves, who have the firstfruits of the Spirit, groan inwardly as we wait eagerly for our adoption as sons, the redemption of our bodies. [24] For in this hope we were saved. But hope that is seen is no hope at all. Who hopes for what he already has? [25] But if we hope for what we do not yet have, we wait for it patiently. [26] In the same way, the Spirit helps us in our weakness. We do not know what we ought to pray for, but the Spirit himself intercedes for us with groans that words cannot express. [27] And he who searches our hearts knows the mind of the Spirit, because the Spirit intercedes for the saints in accordance with God's will. [28] And we know that in all things God works for the good of those who love him, who have been called according to his purpose. [29] For those God foreknew he also predestined to be conformed to the likeness of his Son, that he might be the firstborn among many brothers. [30] And those he predestined, he also called; those he called, he also justified; those he justified, he also glorified. [31] What, then, shall we say in response to this? If God is for us, who can be against us? [32] He who did not spare his own Son, but gave him up for us all—how will he not also, along with him, graciously give us all things? [33] Who will bring any charge against those whom God has chosen? It is God who justifies. [34] Who is he that condemns? Christ Jesus, who died—more than that, who was raised to life—is at the right hand of God and is also interceding for us. [35] Who shall separate us from the love of Christ? Shall trouble or hardship or persecution or famine or nakedness or danger or sword? [36] As it is written: "For your sake we face death all day long; we are considered as sheep to be slaughtered." [37] No, in all these things we are more than conquerors through him who loved us. [38] For I am convinced that neither death nor life, neither angels nor demons, neither the present nor the future, nor any powers, [39] neither height nor depth, nor anything else in all creation, will be able to separate us from the love of God that is in Christ Jesus our Lord. (Romans 8).